Joe,

Thank you so much for your support. May the Grace of God surround your every step!

Isaiah 61

AF327307

Out Of The Ashes

The Anderson Story

Acknowledgements

I want to take the time on the onset to thank some very special people. What makes up our success is the sum of the people that surround us. I am so fortunate to have incredible people around me that made this project a reality.

Elijah Tindall. Thank you for pushing me to do this project. You convinced me that I could do this. Together with your help, guidance, and creativity we put together a wonderful project. It would not have happened without you. The journey was long, and you endured with great patience and believed in me and this project with an unwavering faith. Thank You!

Amy Anderson. You are an incredible gift from God and an amazing blessing to my life. When I did not think we would ever make it to the end of this project, you helped and encouraged me to finish. I thank all my children: Abigail, Alexa, Alec, Adam, and Ayven. Each one of you are so special to my heart. Your mother and I love you deeply and know that you are world changers in your own way. You are part of the story and we pray every day that God is leading you by His divine grace.

Aubrey and Allie Anderson. Your testimony of God's faithfulness is so impactful. What you have overcome is going to touch so many lives. Your continued steadfast and unwavering faith in God almighty is so encouraging. I love watching God expand your families and build dreams that are going to impact the world. You are incredible!

Dedria Bryan. Your journey is so awe inspiring. Your continued pursuit of God and His lovingkindness has been a joy for me to watch. Your sincere compassion for your children and the restoration that God has brought to you, is such a testimony. Whitney and Heston, I am so proud of who you have become and all that you are inspiring to do and be.

Don and Carrol Anderson. Mom and Dad, you are great builders of faith. Your encouragement and strength are so powerful.

You never stopped walking in faith. Your trust in God never wavered and for that I am thankful for all that you do every day for each member of our family.

Faith Center Fellowship. Church family, you are incredible! You amaze me every week by your devotion and encouragement for what God has called us to be and become.   As a church we are carrying the mission of loving people and impacting the world. We see you each week walk in that mission. Together we are seeing God do incredible things.   Thank you for believing in us and this project.

Foreword

Every now and then, a book comes along that deeply and divinely inspires. This is such a book. It is the amazing story of how to overcome the sudden and unexpected loss of family.

Everyone is faced at times with loss and disappointment, and this family has certainly had way more than their share.

Yet, at each turn they chose to focus more on where they were, to look to a God that has a hope and a future not just for them personally, but for others well.

I so encourage you to read the overcoming success story of this amazing family, when faced with worst.... achieved the best. God's grace is still truly amazing.

Joe McGee

Joe McGee Ministries

Tulsa, OK

One would think that naming a team "Red Devils" would indicate something negative (and in most places, it may), but not here. You see, THIS is Northwest Oklahoma. Around these parts, there are two major things that people seem to believe in, God and Football, and not always in that order. Some have called this region the "Belt Buckle" of the Bible Belt. And since that is the case, most parents don't give the local Ringwood School football team's name a second thought. One could even argue that it is the belief of God that allows the name. See, unlike a lot of people who claim to be Christian now days, this is a community who embraces the fact that, if there truly is a God, then there surely is a devil if not, why would God's word talk about him so much and, he is red.

No one ever seemed to bring it up, but if they did, all the former statements could serve as good argument. The name Red Devils was not an issue, because, once again, if there is anything the majority of people in Northwest Oklahoma believe in, it is God and football...and both are much more powerful than the devil.

Like many communities in this region of the United States, to Oklahomans, football is not just an extracurricular activity, it is a rite of passage. The principles of this game help establish a young man's character from one of an irresponsible boy, to that of an accountable man. The plays focus on not just doing things right, and as a result, creating a path of non-resistance, but rather digging in deep and pushing harder when resistance knocks you completely out of breath and off of your feet.

Football allows one to understand that every winning team needs a coach. A person who isn't afraid to get in their faces and let them know that there is a perspective in which they can't see, but if they listen and follow the instructions of someone who has been there hundreds of times before, they have a chance at moving forward. But it is not just a coach that a winning team relies on. Football proves the fact that there is a need for cheerleaders in our lives. People who, even if (and especially when), we seem to be making bad choices, will not just speak words of encouragement to us, but rally others to do so as well.

This is Football. This is Oklahoma. And this, at a middle school field hosting Ringwood's Red Devils, is where our story begins. But before we get to the game, let's take a moment and reflect on this particular day. October 9, 2000 was a day filled with plenty of activity and, as the near future would reveal, life altering choices for the Anderson family. Most parents can relate to the busyness of morning preparation. Work, school and extra- curricular activities seem to fill up the day planner almost immediately. Each have within them things that reach out to us demanding that they take priority over the others.

The Anderson's, consisting of 5 members, Dad, Monte, Mom, Mary, Austin, the oldest son (15) ...a seemingly, natural leader and unmistakenly the boss over his two younger siblings, Aubrey and Allie. Aubrey, 11 years old, is full of life and uses that energy on a daily basis on his quest to become an athletic superstar.

Allie on the other hand, seems content with her ability to melt hearts and make people smile by simply entering the room. Her tiny, 5year-old stature, mixed with the bright blonde hair, somehow made her blue eyes shine right through the fog of a stressful day. This combination of characters all in one house, made for a family full of life, passion and most of all love. There have been many examples of what true love looks like, the Anderson's are most assuredly among those role models.

Monte is a founding pastor of Faith Center. A thriving community church in Meno, Oklahoma. Meno is located on Highway 412. With its proximity to major highways, leading to surrounding communities and cities, this is considered to be a lifeline to Northwest Oklahoma, and Monte's church sat smack dab in the middle.

The churches name accurately described the core, central theme of the Anderson family, Faith. The foundational principle of God's Word that causes one to lean into God and trust Him with all that they have, regardless of the circumstances that come in and out of our lives. As a Pastor and communicator, Monte possessed a natural charisma that caused the Word of God to vibrantly, leap from the pages of the Bible and into the lives of the listener. It wasn't uncommon for people to drive over 50 miles to come listen as he used his words like tools, forming verbal illustrations that drove home simplistic, life application of God's Word. Faith Center brought not only restoration and life to the members of its congregation, but also to the very structure they met in. The building sat as an abandoned school. A place that, in its past, helped train and condition the minds of youth, and preparing adolescents for upcoming tests that would be given.

Elementary preparing for Middle-School. Middle-School preparing for High School and High-School preparing for College...that is the nature of a school. To equip you for your current life, while preparing you and pushing you toward your future. It seems only right that the old school building would now be graduating to a higher call and purpose. Not only would it be used for equipping people for their current life, but it would prepare them for their eternal future. Faith Center brought this building back to life. For Monte, the amount of dedication and extensive time he spent serving people was simply a biproduct result and natural response to the passion his church drew out of him. Monte truly loved his church, and his church felt the same about him.

Mary's presence was a reminder to all that Monte was not alone when it came to charisma in the Anderson family. Mary was not only a caring person, but her ability to translate a loving spirit attracted people to her like a magnet. If there were ever a book written on energy, Mary Anderson would surely be the author.

Her faith and dedication to serving people was outstanding. Gathering others around her to accomplish helping those in need was very natural to her. If our lives were given an anthem, hers would state, "Come on, we can help. Let's get in there and get it done!" Mary would spend her days on the go, for the most part, full of life. This October day was not proving to be any different, in terms of busyness. Her schedule would easily dictate and consume her day if she didn't take control of it first...so, she did.

Like most attentive Pastors and fathers, in the midst of serving people, Monte's day was full of choices. Who would be touched first?

What need would rise to the top and take priority over the already towering stack waiting for pastoral counsel, resolve and direction? But first, breakfast.

"Aubrey, your brother has a junior varsity game at home. Yours is away, and I have to work late today so I don't know if I can make it to your game," said Monte, as he walked through his kitchen, passing his neutrally responsive middle child.

Aubrey's reaction was well within his usual, shyly delivered, character...complete with head nod and all.

"Are you okay with that?" pressed Monte, trying to nudge a cognitive verbal response much like any parent with an 11-year-old has experienced.

"Yes," Aubrey replied in a sheepish manner, all while holding his head in place to face directly at the floor and shrugging his shoulders. It was with that conclude that the family dispersed into their various directions. Schools, Church and meetings. This day had plenty of finish lines to cross.

If you ever spend time with a Pastor, you will quickly learn that change to the schedule is one of the only consistent things to expect. One phone call can re-direct an entire day, sometimes even the whole week. This would drive most people crazy, but not Monte. He exuded an ability to step into any unexpected situation and seem as if he had planned and prepared for every detail. He knew how to roll with the punches, as it were. His natural charisma mixed with the amount of time he spent grounding himself in God's Word, caused his counsel to others to be received with open arms. Monte possessed a special "something." The thing that makes people stop and take notice the moment he steps into the room. His smile lighting up the darkest of atmospheres and released a sense of comfort and encouragement.

Although the elements of pressure and busyness were no different, on this day, something else seemed to be. It was hard to pinpoint, but something was stirring in the heart of this pastor. It was reminiscent of the stories you hear of animals that sense an earthquake before it takes place. Their inner senses trigger warnings to their consciousness. The restlessness causing others to notice that something is different, but, because it is in the unseen future, no one knows what, or why.

Though we all say, "family first," the fact is, most of us have struggled to define WHEN it is okay to drop everything else and go support one of our children. It becomes even more difficult where multiple children are involved. Once you make the decision to put work on hold, which child do you go support? This is a challenging question, not just for a Pastor, but for every dad, mother and parent.

What is the most important thing we possess? Is it not the family that God has blessed our lives with? The obvious answer that springs out of us is yes. Yet, if we are honest about it, most of us are still, very easily distracted by the external things capturing our attention. It is not that they are bad things, nor is it that they would produce a negative result when given our focus. The issue is always a matter of priority. Are these things pulling me away from what is important? At what point do you say, "this can wait, and this cannot?"

The stirring in Monte began to set a challenge within his heart, redirecting the choices of what would become priority for the day. Places to be, work to be done, another junior varsity game of his oldest son or Aubrey's, away, grade school football game. There was also the option to just unplug and go home, he surely could use the few hours to relax and rest, but that was not the kind of man he was. After a few moments of thought, he settled on his choice and resolved to stop what he was doing, make the 45-minute drive to the grade school game, and watch his youngest son, Aubrey, play football.

Climbing into his car, he pauses to take in the cooling air. Oklahomans know that there is a brisk chill the evening ushers in during football season. It encourages you to make your way to the team of volunteers working in the vending room and purchase a warm plate of nachos. And while you're there, you might as well buy a hot dog, popcorn, hot chocolate and a Frito-chili pie...you know, so you don't have to come back later. Oh, and a pack of M&M's. Those that don't care for the cool weather are not out of luck completely, because, as the saying goes, "If you don't like the weather, stick around, it will change by the end of the day."

As Monte pulled into Waynoka, Oklahoma, he found the perfect spot to park his car. One of the unique things about some football fields in rural Oklahoma is that you can park right by the field and watch the game from your car. That was the case on this night as Monte slowed to a stop and put his car in park at the end zone of the Waynoka Railroader football field.

Aubrey played tight end for the Red Devils 8-man football team. They were successful in working the football up the field a few yards at a time. Periodically they would pull out an option play and hopefully advance more than just a few yards.

The Ringwood Red Devils are now on the 30-yard line, advancing toward the goal. Overall, the game was going well. The players huddled, and a play is called. Aubrey's excitement is elevated due to the fact that this play will be a pass to his position. His anxious yet excited expression was shielded by the face guard on his helmet as the team broke from the huddle and positioned themselves at the line. The coolness of the air provided just the right temperature to cause a smoky breath effect as they exhaled. That, mixed with the contrast of the bright lights shining against the dark sky, makes one disregard the fact that these are just young boys playing a game. It's as if we, for a brief moment, catch a glimpse of the warrior nature of the man they will become in life. We encourage them to dig deep, to push hard, and to keep fighting.

If only we could maintain that spirit later in life when they need that encouragement as adults. Perhaps our excitement in these moments is not just that we are cheering for someone we know, but that we are cheering at all. Maybe we catch a glimpse of the person we too are supposed to be. A person who encourages others in their time of need. A person who gives rather than takes. Could it be that, this feeling of excitement is connected to our actions just as much as it is to theirs?

The scene is broken as the center snaps the ball. All players take action as their eyes shift quickly around the field to pinpoint the location of the ball. The quarterback quickly slides back as Aubrey moves into motion. He rushes toward the end of the line and shifts directions down the field. The quarterback continues to move back, sets himself, and throws the ball. Looking over his shoulder, Aubrey sees the throw, accelerates his pace, reaches up and catches the ball. He is met by a Waynoka Railroader in a tackle, just short of the goal line.

Out of the many cheering voices at that moment, one stood out, "Great job Aubrey!" At that moment, as Aubrey looked down the field, his disappointment of not reaching the goal line quickly faded. The excitement of seeing his dad's car parked beyond the end zone was a very welcomed feeling. Even though his response was one of a muted nature that morning in the kitchen, the fact remained, that it did matter whether or not dad made it to the game. And, in true Monte character, he did.

As Aubrey jogs back to the huddle for the next play, his eyes scanned the sidelines in search of his father. Monte's voice, cutting through the crowd of other parents, Aubrey finally found what he was looking for, his father, cheering him on from the sidelines. Monte's ability to project volume far surpassed the average and could easily span the length of a football stadium...after all, he did communicate for a living.

Although Monte's was the one that stood out to Aubrey, I am sure that each young man out on that field felt the same when their father broke the silence and cheered for them. There is something special about the present voice of a father. Its immediate recognition solidifies the fact that, "I am loved." And that love resonates in the heart of the child.

Just like in the game that night, there are many voices speaking to us all at once. Remember, there was an entire side of the field in opposition to Aubrey moving forward. They, unlike his father, were most likely releasing words that would be discouraging to him.

The same goes for all of us. There will be voices that speak into our hearts on a constant basis. The question is, what voice are you listening to? Jesus unfolds a truth for us in the gospel of Matthew, chapter 10. He reveals himself as the speaking shepherd, and all other voices will be that of thieves. They will steal from our lives. His encouragement is to not follow the other voice. God truly does lead by

His voice. It can be in a still small voice, leading and nudging from the inside. The Bible defines this as, the Holy Spirit bearing witness with our spirit. His voice can also be spoken through the written Word of God. It comes alive in our hearts and we see the direction that we need to go. These are just two of the ways He speaks to us, but the point and fact is, He is speaking. The vital question for each of us to answer is, are you listening?

Aubrey's run back to the huddle was one with excitement in his heart and a strength to continue in this game. What could be more empowering to him than a surprise appearance from his dad and hearing his voice cheering him on!

The next snap of the football came, and the Ringwood Red Devils marched into the end zone to complete the touch down. In the end, Aubrey's team won the ball game that night, but in reality, a larger win took place. A dad stopped in the midst of a long list of things to get accomplished and made it to his son's game. Monte paused in the midst of all the tasks and measured their importance. He took action on the fact that the greatest of all the priorities was that of his family. Nothing was as much of a gift and blessing to him as his family, and he, in this moment, made that the factor to dictate his decision.

The outcome of the game had very little significance in the grand scheme of wins that night. The fact that he was there for his son was what really mattered. Aubrey saw his face and heard his voice. Monte, once again, set an example to all who watched, that he was a dad first, and a pastor second. He was an encourager of life to his children first, and it showed. The gleam that sparkled from Monte's eyes when he looked into the faces of his children caused a contagious smile. A smile led by his face, and lovingly spread to anyone within a visual proximity. There is no faking the true, loving expression that comes upon the face of one looking into the eyes of their children. In Monte's mind, he correctly identified, that there is no better place to be at this moment, than right here, right now.

The game ended, and the Ringwood Red Devils once again take a win. Their walk across the field was victorious. Monte patted his son, number 84 on the back, in a gesture of healthy pride. After passersby congratulated Aubrey, he and dad walk toward the car parked at the end zone. A walk that was full of heart felt encouragement, love and pride. Monte's heart was full, knowing that the priority choice he made to put his son first placed him right where he was supposed to be. Aubrey had a good game and the love and encouragement of his father was icing on this victorious cake.

Priorities, when executed, establish an environment of encouragement and love. This reality, when lived out, goes far beyond words. Right priorities produce a righteous presence in our homes and lives. It always takes great sacrifice to execute the priorities of God first and family second. It takes strong conviction to say, "these things can wait, and I need to be there." It takes true fortitude to push through the tight times in life and communicate, "I have priorities that must be fulfilled." When on the other side of the conviction and fortitude it takes to execute these priorities, we find that the reward is one of a secure family. A family that knows they are important.

We all thrive in an atmosphere of right priorities. You give me a family that is set in right priorities, and I will give you a family that is secure in who they are; a family that thrives. Today, Monte Anderson, a man of love and compassion for others, shifted his time and made a priority decision. His choices, this day, made him full of life.

Monte and Aubrey climbed into the car, started it up and began their 45-minute journey back home to Ringwood. Aubrey, tired from the game and Monte reflecting on the day he drove onward. Neither one knowing that this ride home, would forever change the course of the Anderson family.

Anyone who has lived in a rural area can attest to the fact that there is nothing quite like the atmosphere of the evening drive. Most nights consist of a sunset that fades from clear, sky blue, to a soft purplish hue blending and transitioning into what appears to be a mixture between orange and pink. If there are clouds in the sky, they ascend the surrounding colors by contrasting with a deep, darkening grey. The sky, starlit, which, in its mystical beauty, tends to draw out the most internal of thoughts.

It is as if the star's level of brightness has been turned up by an unseen, heavenly dimmer switch. Mixed with the deep, black backdrop of the evening sky, once experienced, these nights are not easily forgotten. The absence of being surrounded by rushing traffic allows you to unwind and relax as you navigate your vehicle down the narrow, yet familiar roads. The wonderful stage of God's design unfolds and reveals itself clearly as you sit back, take a deep breath and gaze upon it through the windshield.

As Monte Anderson takes in the view, he continues his drive back home from the victorious elementary football game. Aubrey, 11 years old, a young boy, all too quickly, becoming a young man, has already faded into sleep mode. Mid-game adrenaline has worn off and exhaustion has caught up to him. Silently, he rests in the passenger seat as Monte drives them toward their home in Ringwood. Monte's reflection on life in those moments, caused him to, once again, think about what God has done, not just for him, but for those he loves.

Monte and Mary's decision to take on the responsibility and call of pioneering Faith Center Fellowship was not one that came without difficulty. It seemed to be the common, unattractive nature of people to not want to forget a person's past. This point became more relevant as they discovered that a large part of Monte's Pastoral call was specific to his hometown area of Meno, Oklahoma. For the Anderson family, and Monte, in this case, there was much history here.

It is worthy of noting that, in His Word, the Bible declares, *"The giftings and callings of God, are without repentance."* Meaning,

He is not going to repent or say He is sorry for the call He places on people. It is amazing how much God continues to un-apologetically, call men and women into His ministry, regardless of anyone else's opinion. It is with that call, that Monte and Mary decided to stand united, and pastor this church.

In a town population of under 200, and a county of right at 6,000 people, their dedication led the congregation in a numeric growth, over a 10- year span, from 6 people, to over 200 on a weekly basis. That number is a good reflection of the impact they were having on their community. Any pastor, in any region, would be thrilled with the knowledge that they are reaching beyond 3 percent of the population in their area, but his passion went far beyond the local region around him. The desire to make a global impact resounded in his spirit. This call, mixed with his heart and ethic for working hard, resulted in churches and orphanages being built in Guatemala and Nicaragua, ministering in Costa Rica and El Salvador, training pastors and leaders in the underground church in Vietnam and helping put water in villages in Cambodia and areas of Nicaragua. In addition to all this, he was also engaged in building a School of Ministry on the Isle of Youth off the Cuban mainland. His dedication to always make room for people drove him forward, and on this night, that dedication found him scooting things over to make room for his son.

A family bond was no small thing among the Anderson family. Monte's upbringing was filled with being surrounded by faith and family. His parents, Don and Carrol, a couple who can trace their relationship back to meeting at a high school basketball game in 1956 and married four years later, were both highly committed to filling the house with a visible pursuit of God. Their time was consumed with the responsibilities of work and raising the Anderson kids. In addition to Monte, who was born in 1961 in Canyon, Texas, they parented younger brother, Cody, and sister Dedria. By this time, Cody was also working as a staff member at a church in Oklahoma City. Dedria was happily establishing her home and raising a family in East Texas.

From parents to children, the landscape of the Anderson family was set with a backdrop of faith in God and a firm foundation in His infallible Word. A richness of love and support exuded from and surrounded them all. Not to be mistaken, the Anderson family would never pitch themselves as perfect or better than anyone else, they had their share of real-life parenting issues to deal with, just like the rest of us.

When asked, it doesn't take too much prompting until Don gladly shares a story of the time a local Sheriff brought Monte home to their door. Hearing the knock, Don recalls making his way from the living room and passing a window where he saw the Sheriff's patrol car sitting in the driveway. Upon opening the front door, he met the sight of his, sheepish statured, teenage son standing shoulder to elbow beside the Sheriff on the porch. Back in those days, if you were caught speeding or running a stop sign, your license would be taken from you and returned when you paid the fine. The question Don had for the Sheriff, a personal friend (both a good and bad thing, depending on the situation)

"Why didn't you just take his license? You didn't have to bring him here in your car, did you?"

"I did take his license, Don...yesterday, when I pulled him over. Today was a whole new citation."

It would appear that Monte had been less than revealing with the truth the night before, and life, as it always is, was more than willing to uncover hidden truths to unsuspecting parents of teenagers. Though Monte already knew Jesus, he was about to meet him, yet again.

As Monte drove forward on this clear Oklahoma night, he was well aware of the fact that, not everyone can look through a windshield and see what God has done with their life. There are times that as we look through the windshield of our own journey, we may not like the view.

The curves, hills, and potholes may cause us to be hesitant in moving forward. Abrupt stops, obstacles, clouded views and even dead ends, have made us reject the thought of our future having a positive potential. Truth be told, we must admit that we all have fallen into this category at some point. We have all faced struggles and challenges in life. There are seasons, these struggles have caused our view to become unclear. Part of Monte's past brings this reality to the fore front. Perhaps it was the fact that, in his early 20's, living for God was not part of his life plan, that made his reflections on this night, looking out of his windshield, so beautiful. God had stepped in, as He often does, and changed his view on everything. The cancelation of negative thoughts of himself, struggling financially, hitting the party scene and desperately looking for work with nothing more than a High School diploma, brought him freedom. Though he and Mary met while in this season of life, things began to change. They emerged from the drinking and party scene to a life of stability. Monte finally did find good employment and, more importantly, over time, fully surrendered complete Lordship over his life to Jesus. He let go of the secret and small things that kept him from being 100 percent IN. Mary did the same.

There is a big difference in saying we give Jesus the complete control and Lordship over our lives, and actually doing so. Most Christians are familiar with embracing the concept of having a savior yet resisting the Lordship part. We are happy to take the "You are forgiven" part, it's the "Now go and sin no more" line that brings a challenge. It challenges our lifestyle. It uproots the weeds that choke out the healthy things God wants to grow from the seeds His word has planted. It is always a personal choice. Over a season of time, Monte and Mary made the right choices. These personal decisions made a public difference in both of them. His view on this night reflected all of this, and that is why he could be at peace.

This drives home the statement "Beauty is in the eye of the beholder". It is what happens on the inside of us that determines our view of the outside. Changing the windshield does not change our perspective, changing our perspective is what changes everything. Monte and Mary's view was changed because of their decision to change internally. It did not resolve all the hills and curves, but it did cause them to adjust the way they navigated through them. They now lived differently.

We each have this same opportunity. For some, it may go even further. You notice those who are stuck in the past. Whether it be the aging man who still refers to the time he was quarterback in high school, and they almost took state, or the bitterness of a person holding unforgiveness against another for an offense of the past, you can identify that some people focus on what is behind them, more than what is before them. For these people, the rearview mirror becomes the focus. They continue to move forward, but the problem is, when we move forward while looking behind us, we eventually end up getting or causing hurt. Though there is a giant windshield framing our future and its journey, our focus becomes on something very small...a view of our past.

This is problematic in so many ways. Not only is it that we don't like to see what the current and future view is, we refuse to acknowledge it. Too much time is spent referring to our past, even good experiences of our past can cause us to not move forward. Eventually, it is impossible to continue to look at what is behind us without seeing a failure of some sort. Once that happens, we become emotionally surrounded by the obstacles, curves and wreckage. We will, overtime, just stop moving forward at all. Many people are in this position. The reality of the past has paralyzed them from moving forward. Once again, the attitude toward the things we see on the outside are only a reflection of the perspective we see them with.

If we were shrunk down and placed inside a blender after it successfully chopped fruit, our view would be very smudged and blocked with the splatter of the fruit that has been blended. From our perspective, the entire rest of the kitchen would be a fruit smeared mess. But on the outside of that blender the reality may be that the kitchen was spotless and clean. Our perspective is what we believe, even though truth may be the complete opposite. All we can focus on is the mess we see from our position. Perhaps it's time to, either accept that we are allowing things to cause us to only see the negative or change our position. Monte did both, and because of it, this drive home, he was full of gratefulness and reflection on all that God had done for him, regardless of the suddenly shifting view outside his windshield that was about to change everything.

Out of the Ashes *Chapter 3* - It Just Happened

Without warning, from left to right, a shadow suddenly crosses the front of Monte's car. The silent calm of the night was broken by headlights shining into his eyes, illuminating his face inside the driver's seat of his small green sports car. An oncoming vehicle continued to merge across the center line of the highway, and directly into what seemed like the only car within miles…Monte's. The collision was a sudden, head on hit. When the car did come to a stop, it had found itself resting upside down on its roof.

Young Aubrey is abruptly wakened from his sleep inside the vehicle. He does his best to understand what is happening. When he last closed his eyes, all was sound, all was normal, and now, quite literally, his world has been turned upside down. He shakes his head and squints his eyes in hopes to gain a better perspective, or perhaps even, wake up from this horrific nightmare, but clarity only brought more hurt. His desire to breathe causes him to take sudden, sporadic gasps for air, each of which causing a shooting pain, much like a knife being thrust through his entire body. His legs are noticeably injured and resting under him as he sits upright on the inside roof of the upside-down vehicle. Nothing about this makes sense to him. There is a quietness and stillness about this moment as he looks around in the darkness. Through the smoke and rubble, he sees his dad.

Aubrey, in an attempt to get out of the car, shifts from side to side. Trying to avoid the fact that the only exit for him would be to climb out over his father. He begs for a response from Monte, but none can be found. Aubrey falls outside the vehicle, and still, there is no response. No approaching vehicles, no help in sight and hope is fleeting his 11-year-old heart and mind. Aubrey painfully forces himself to stand on his injured legs. With great pain, he begins taking steps, into the darkness of this once peaceful Oklahoma night, hopefully searching for something or someone, and yet, there was no response.

The driver from the other vehicle, strangely enough, was also a pastor. He was driving home in a loaned vehicle, since his was damaged in an accident just a few hours prior to this one. His church was in a neighboring small community. Though the two had never met, this Pastor was familiar with Monte's name and the work they had done at Faith Center Fellowship. It would forever be the case that their meeting place would be a tragic one. A collision caused by what the Pastor describes as an unavoidable swerve due to a passing deer on the highway. One deer, one reaction, two cars and one hurting young man, looking onward for help. It just happened.

An accident. Nothing intentional by anyone. An accident that cannot be explained by anyone. Theology makes attempts to explain accidents by using terms such as destiny and sovereignty. While we do not question the sovereignty of God, nor deny that His Word states that the days of man are numbered, we are of the belief that He is continuously speaking by His voice instructions of direction, "Stop, don't go, turn here, don't turn there." These types of things are certainly within His ability. But there are times when we miss the mark of perfection when it comes to following His direction. It is in these moments that we can find ourselves, right in the middle of an accident. Not just in a vehicle, but in every area of our lives. That being said, we know that there are differing opinions on these types of things.

Our goal is not to debate theology, but rather, to reveal the belief stance of the Anderson family. Regardless of where any of us fall in our perspective of why accidents happen, the fact remains, they still happen. When they do, theology will not rescue you, only a personal relationship with Jesus Christ can prepare us for such events.

As vehicles begin to pull up on the accident, someone sees Aubrey in the distance. His confusion still causing disarray as he stumbles, step by step into darkness. The driver of the vehicle pulls to a stop, places the car in park and runs to him. As a coat is placed over his shoulders, this young man, still wearing the football jersey from the game he and his dad just left only minutes ago, collapses. He falls to the ground abruptly as the pain from the broken ankle he had been walking on set in. The adrenaline caused from the shock of trauma was wearing off and reality was becoming more painful. Less than 2 miles from their home, Monte and Aubrey's journey was interrupted.

It just happened.

Being a small town, it didn't take long before word got out that Monte had been in an accident and phones began to ring. In communities like this, you don't think twice about doing what you can to help, you just go and see what needs to be done. And, it was with that kind of character, that neighbors quickly made their way to the crash site. Someone calls Mary to make sure she was informed, but, to this point, this was the first she had heard. Grabbing her oldest son, Austin and her 5-year-old baby girl, Allie, they rushed down the highway directly toward the flashing lights. At the same time, Don and Carrol, having also been made aware through a phone call, were making the 6-mile journey from their home to the accident.

When Mary arrives, she senses that Monte is not going to be okay. By this time, the Emergency Medical Technicians have placed Aubrey onto a board and have him strapped down. His hearing bombarded by voices of family members franticly trying to absorb the situation. His eyes, shifting back and forth to gain clarity and understanding of what is happening, find a paramedic as he asks, "Where is my dad?"

"He is being tended to," replied the medic.

Austin rushes out of the car and on to the scene. This 5'10, fifteen-year-old makes his way to the wreckage of his father's car. He is standing among a huddle of others doing everything they can to help, but there is no response.

Austin's personality was never one to ask for permission. When action was needed, he carried an inner confidence which gave him permission to get involved. This tenacity would prove to serve him well later in life as a Marine.

In this moment, he scans the scene, and there are two sights being taken in. Both overwhelming. One, his younger brother, strapped down inside the back of an ambulance. His face, noticeably scared and lonely. His eyes staring at the ceiling of the Ambulance interior. And two, looking beyond the emergency vehicles, was his dad's car. Upside down, mangled and surrounded by dust, the car seemed so out of place. This is the same car that Monte was teaching him to drive in. The laughs, caused by the inexperience of popping the clutch too soon, would not be heard again in this vehicle. The times of listening to music and hearing his dad's favorite songs while sitting in the green sports car together were no more. His secret hope that this car would be the one he got when he turned 16, was no longer relevant. It has happened. An accident that cannot be taken back. A life that is taken away from the Anderson family.

"Get back to the car! Allie is by herself," cried Mary, bringing Austin back to the reality of this moment.

The gaze of his and others hearing Mary's instruction, turned to the Anderson's Lincoln town car. Lights shone all around it, and, from the rear window, a small face surrounded with golden blonde hair appeared. 5-year-old Allie was taking in a life changing moment as she sat in the back of this car. This would not be the last time Allie's life will be changed and redirected while in this same environment, but it was the first. And this, as all know, is too much for a child to handle.

Austin makes his way back to the car to be present for his younger sister. As he does, Monte's parents arrive to the scene. Though their names are Don and Carrol, the family has always called them "Papa" and "Annie". Annie walks up, taken back by what she is seeing. While movement and plenty of activity was happening, no one was attending to her son. Monte had already been pronounced dead at the scene. Thoughts of confusion rush as she tries to maintain composure. Knowing that she can still add help and comfort to Austin and Allie, she painfully made her way to the family car. All three sit in the quiet of night, looking ahead with blank stares as emptiness begins to flood their hearts.

Papa urgently, yet reluctantly walks over to where Monte is laying. He kneels down next to him, slides his hands under his son's head, and holds it for the last time. The heart of this father is broken. Nothing, at this point can be done to bring him back.

No words contain enough emotion or meaning for this moment, so none can be spoken. It just happened.

Out of the Ashes *Chapter 4 - The Gathering*

Carrol, whose heart is in a state of complete dismay by what has just taken place, sits at the scene of the accident. Lights from the Highway Patrol vehicle were still flashing as they waited on the wrecker service to complete the task of clearing the scene. Pieces of, what was only hours ago, a complete green sports car, lay sprawled alongside this Oklahoma highway. Impossible as it was to believe or accept, her oldest son was gone.

"NO" Carrol cried, as she looks out of the window of her car. "NO, NO, NO, God, how can this be?"

The question came from the depths of her spirit and soul. Grief was setting in quickly. Her observance over the wreckage was interrupted by a tapping on her window. Startled by the unexpected sound, she switches her attention to the source of the tap, a family friend stands at the driver's side door leaning in. Blankly, Carrol starred, in a transition between internal emotion and current reality, she finally comprehends who this is. Ira, being a dear friend to Monte, had heard about the accident and made his way from his home in Enid, Oklahoma. The 30-mile drive seemed to last for hours. He had to come see what has happened with his friend...his Pastor.

"Carrol, can I help you with anything?" asked Ira.

"I need to go to the Fairview Hospital," she replied.

Ira, without hesitation, responded, "I will drive you."

There were two hospitals involved in hosting the Anderson family on this tragic night. The first was St. Mary's Hospital in Enid Oklahoma, where young Aubrey was transported to treat his ankle injury. The second, was Fairview Hospital, where Monte was taken. There was a specific reason for this divide... a very painful reason.

Fairview Hospital was home to the local Morgue.

The fact that his body was being sent here seemed like the unwelcomed period on sentence that could not be erased. The bond between a mother and her son is one of deep compassion. Even in the hectic confusion and chaos being handed to Mary this night, she still found herself being drawn to go where her son was being sent. And, without hesitation, Carrol did the same. Both much like Mary in the Bible, being present for their son, no matter what state he was in. And onward they drove.

Pulling away from the lights, into the darkness and quiet of the night, Carrol began to reflect on her son's life. Carrol was a woman of faith and prayer. She and Don were vitally responsible for the strong faith that the entire family had established themselves in. In this moment, that faith was shaken. Her ability to find the right words to pray was becoming difficult. The English language contained none for such a situation. That is when she started to draw on her spiritual language.

Being a person filled with the Holy Spirit, Carrol drew upon the promise of God's Word, to build up her most Holy Faith. Thanking God that, even in our weakness, the Holy Spirit begins to strengthen us. In this moment, that is what she needed. A faith that is Holy and perfect from God. The God that has always proven Himself faithful to her family. She began to become fervent in prayer, preparing her for what she was about to see. A sight, no mother should ever have her eyes opened to.

As the moments passed on their drive, several close family friends had arrived at the Fairview Hospital. As Carrol walked into the hospital, this gathering of friends, already considered to be close as family to the Anderson's, embraced her. They decided to walk united into where Monte was, surrounded the gurney that held his body, and pray for a miracle. For a moment, they turned their sorrow into a mountain of faith. They continued to pray, declaring life into Monte's body and complete healing over his neck, which had been broken during the crash. They were fervent in their prayers. To some, even in the Christian faith, this may sound foolish, but to others, it is only a natural response to the faith we embrace.

The Word of God is full of miracles. The blind gained sight, the crippled began to walk, diseased made whole, and the dead raised. There are some in the Christian faith that would never even venture to that way of thinking. Not to the Anderson family. These are a people of faith. On the mission field, they themselves had been first hand witness to God working miracles as a result of the action they took to believe Him at His Word. If He said it, He can do it, and If He did it once, He could surely do it again. In this moment, nothing changed. Monte always said, "If you know that I am face to face with Jesus, do NOT ask me to come back."

Face to face with Jesus. This is what we, that are followers of Christ, are all living for. Waiting to be in the presence of our Savior. Coming to worship the King of Kings and the Lord of Lords in the very throne room of Heaven, being described in the book of Revelation, chapter 21, as a city with 12 gates, each made of pearl, streets as pure gold in transparent likeliness. It is a difficult place for most of us to wrap our minds around. In the Gospel of John, chapter 14, Jesus describes heaven as having mansions. Revelation's description indicates that of an individual beauty. A place where every tear is wiped away. No more death, mourning, sorrow or pain will be present, as these were never God's plan for us. Revelation 22 declares that there will be no more night, because God's glory produces continual light. It goes on to say that there will be no more curse, and, for the first time, we will see God. The throne of God and Lamb of God, our Savior and King will be in the city. Knowing that His Word states, "to die, is gain," Carrol and the gathering of friends were at peace. Though those left on this side had temporarily lost, Monte had gained. He gained heaven. Carrol gives a kiss on his forehead and whispers, "This is only for a moment, I will see you again in heaven."

Meanwhile, at St. Mary's Hospital in Enid, Oklahoma, there was an ever- increasing gathering of church family, all there to support Mary as she stays to ensure that her son, Aubrey is getting every bit of care that he needed. Don, Monte's father, Mary's father-in-law, waited with her in the Emergency room. After a matter of time, Aubrey was released with a cast upon one ankle and brace on the other. Due to the fact that both ankles incurred damage, Aubrey would have to be in a wheelchair for a season. The weight of his body on the injuries would have prevented him from complete healing. In this moment looking at Aubrey, it is hard to imagine that only hours ago, his life had none of these broken issues. The instructions to "stay off your feet," can be hard to accept. On the inside, we feel like we can stand. We feel strong enough, but there are seasons, not just in our physical life, but our spiritual, mental and emotional, that Jesus, the Great Physician, is instructing us to "stay" or "rest", in order for true healing to take place. This brokenness can either lead to healing, or further pain. Aubrey was at the beginning of that season.

Within the time it took to drive from Oklahoma City to Enid, Uncle Cody, Monte's brother and his wife Amy arrived at the hospital with their daughter Abigail. From the moment he entered the door, he was surrounded by people, from wall to wall, a gathering of caring friends. The pastoral ministry call in him could not ignore the fact that he was looking at not only a dismayed family, but a broken church. Tears flood their eyes and compassionate embraces were being shared all across the room. Cody, stepping into the room where his dad sat, moves forward to embrace his father. Don meets him with open arms. Both exuding bellowing cries. A son, who just lost his big brother, and a father, having been stripped the opportunity to ever embrace his oldest child again, they just cried.

As Cody pulled away from his father, he moved toward Mary and Austin. He is not only witness to, but part of a brokenness that words cannot describe. A moment of pain that the heart will never forget. Each one would embrace each other as if their life depended on it. The strength there, in that moment, was due to the bond of faith and love. This strength would be called upon as a constant resource needed for the difficult times ahead. There was a closeness established in the waiting room of this hospital over the next hour. The gathering of the church and immediate Anderson family members was going through something together, and that something was drawing the best out of them, even in the worst season.

That was testimony of what Monte had built. It was more than a church to gather and worship God, but a house that was full of people who loved God and loved, truly loved each other. They would be more than a group of people who would just gather together to fulfill religious obligation and then leave. They, rather, would be a people who would gather and serve one another, just as Christ serves the church. Jesus died sacrificially for the sins of all mankind. Monte viewed the Church as much more than a gathering place for worship, but a gathering of people who would love one another.   In the midst of a moment of great tragedy, you could see the beauty of the family, and body of Christ, to become strength for one another. We were never designed to go through moments of crisis and tragedy alone. We, like the Anderson's, on this night, all need a gathering of people who will be like family. A gathering of those who give us a reflection of God's strength, comfort and compassion. This night was a beautiful example of the church that Monte loved, in action. This gathering would be something that was evident strength and comfort to the Anderson family.

It is very true that people love to gather in groups and do things with a crowd. There are some that are so introverted in their personality that they could hide out from other people for months and think that was incredible. For the majority of most people, they like to associate and be around other people. It is not about social gatherings or getting hyped up about a certain party. It is, however, about being around people that are genuine in their faith and love of God that is revealed through them. When you ever find a life-giving church and community of faith, you see the beauty of God's love and compassion at work. God always uses people to encourage people. That is the beauty of the Body of Christ. When we are together, we encourage and strengthen each other's faith and love for God. There may be times that we don't want people to be around. But when people that genuinely care, you love to be around those type of people, and this night that is what the Anderson's felt.

Sometimes truth contradicts logic. For example, one would think that the moment something goes from visible to invisible, it loses its effectiveness, but before we just dismiss this to be logical, let's look at truth.

There is a passage in James (4:14) that states, *"Our life is but a vapor/mist."* This indicates that, just like a mist, it fades away. It is here one moment and gone the next. What was once visible is now invisible. We all encounter things that contradict this every day. From hairspray to perfume (or cologne depending on how manly you are). Each of these things are a substance concocted to serve a specific purpose. The hairspray, to hold things in place as long as possible. The perfume, to surround us with a soft, pleasant aroma.

Each is placed in a container to host the substance, after that, the nozzle is placed on the container and this nozzle releases these substances in a spray/mist form. There is, most likely a moment in each of our days, when we spray the mist of one of those substances into the air. Though its purpose is to land on us, there is a short time when you can visibly see the "mist" in mid-air. For some, based on the amount we choose to use, it's a very short moment. But for others, it may be longer. What is unique about this analogy is that the effectiveness of the substance is not based on whether it is visible or not. The effectiveness is based on whether it has been released into the atmosphere. No matter how much purpose the substance has, it can't be served until it is released. The issue then becomes the fact that, the more it is released, the emptier the container becomes.

Like these items I just mentioned, we all contain a "substance." Each of us have a purpose, a special concoction put together for a specific reason. We all have been given these earthly bodies, which serve as containers to host the "substance" of our lives.

Every day we live, we are releasing the mist of our lives into the atmosphere around us. The words we speak, the attitudes our expressions indicate, they all land on the people around us. At this moment, the "mist" of our lives can be visibly seen. It is physically tangible to everyone around. But the fact is, every day we live, the container becomes a bit emptier. There is a moment when each of us will step from the natural realm (the visible), to the eternal realm (the invisible).

Let's remember something very important here. The purpose of the mist I mentioned before is not for the moments it can be seen, but rather for the moments it can't. The effectiveness of the hairspray is that it serves the purpose of holding things in place long after its visibility is gone. The value of the perfume is determined not just by its immediate aroma, but by the length of time it stays in the atmosphere.

This is the same principle that God has placed in each of our lives. Not just to be someone who serves a purpose when we are visible, but long after our visibility has passed. It is important to understand that there will never be a moment when we do not exist. We are created to be eternal. Given this truth, there are two questions we are faced with, 1. "Where will I spend eternity?" 2. "How will the purpose of my life, while I am here on earth (visible mist), continue to make a difference once I step into the eternal realm?"

Let's look at the first question: *"Where will I spend Eternity?"*

John 3:16 is the most quoted verse in the Bible, for good reason. Within His few words, Jesus stated the simplicity of how to activate the rescue plan for mankind. This is the way that you and I can spend eternity in the presence of a loving God. His words were *"For God so loved the world, that He gave His only begotten son, that WHOSOEVER believes on Him, shall not perish, but have eternal life."*

Jesus made it pretty clear here. He was not apologetic about being so specific to the gentleman he told this to. He was direct with this information. A lot people criticize when Christians make these kinds of statements. They feel it is a very closed-minded way to believe. The fact that there is only one way to get to heaven is a bit narrow in thinking for most. It is surprising to me that they are not as "openminded" when it comes to other things. For example, I haven't heard anyone complain about a surgeon being very specific about how they train and go about doing surgeries. They want that doctor to be clear. The same with pilots. I think we would all avoid an airline who hires pilots that feel that there are many different ways to fly a plane. There is no absolute. Why are they closed to this way of thinking about these things? The fact is, they are closed because they value the "mist" more than they do the invisible. Just like most, they are drawn to make decisions based on the temporary rather than the eternal. The problem with that is, "our life is but a mist." It is fading away.

Jesus' plan was stated here to follow:

1.   God loves the world and gave his son (Jesus) for it.

2.   Whoever believes on him (Jesus) shall have eternal life.

Some people hold back on this because they don't understand all the details. If that is you, I would encourage you by saying this, none of us understand all the details.

There is a huge gap between God's level of thinking and ours. It is by faith that we believe and as we do, we get closer to Him and learn more.

Here is the second question: *"How will the purpose of my life, while I am here, continue to make a difference after I step into the eternal realm?"*

The higher the quality of the substance we contain, the longer it lasts after we pass. Unlike the hairspray and perfume examples, we have been given an opportunity to decide the amount of quality our substance is. We have been given the right, by God, to pour in the ingredients. He has made clear in Romans 12:2 that, if we are to fulfill His "perfect will" for our lives, we must fill ourselves with His way of thinking. The only way to do this is to study the way He thinks. The beauty is, we get to use a cheat sheet through the entire test. He has given us His Word. We can literally open it every day and fill ourselves up with the exact ingredients to produce the highest quality substance to release into this world. Our time here can be more than just temporarily visible. We can take actions now that will influence the choices our great-great grandchildren live.

I don't know about you, but I want the substance of the mist I spray into this atmosphere to be so powerful that it creates layers of spiritual truth over my future family members. There is a reason we are still talking about Moses, Joseph and King David. That reason is quality of substance. Like us, each had flaws, each had failures, but each decided to resolve their character and grow closer to God. I look forward to the day, in the eternal realm, that I meet one of these guys. Not because of the visibility I had of their time here on earth, but because of how they chose to live it. It shaped the way I choose to live mine.

Our history is molded and filled by those before us, who's mist continues to serve its purpose. Our mist is slowly passing from visible to invisible. Let's be determined that it will reach far beyond this moment and strengthen the future generations.

Mary, Austin, Aubrey, and Allie would find themselves in Don and Carrol's home. The thought of being in their home without Monte was too much for them to bear at this time. The Don and Carrol Anderson's home was large enough with a basement in it that had a large living room and two bedrooms and a full bathroom. This basement had served as a meeting place for Bible Studies and a place of refuge for ministry on many occasions. At this time, a refuge is what Mary and the children would find. It was not only a place of strength but of love and comfort. There is a shock that is upon the family following the day after the wreck. Decisions would have to be made and everyone is looking for what direction to go in. Cody begins to support in any way possible, and with the details of the funeral awaiting the family, the heaviness is seen on every face and the desperation upon their hearts keeps the family in a quiet state of mind.

The family gathered at the funeral home a day prior to the funeral services for the viewing. Hundreds of people have come to show support and love for the family. Over and over again you would hear people testify of how this rural Oklahoma Pastor had touched their lives in some way. In their condolences, people would try so hard to say something meaningful, and even theological, in hopes that what they said would bring some sense of comfort. Many times, that is the case, it is truly meaningful and has potential to bring levels of comfort. However, there are a few that create anger more than comfort.

Austin did not deal with the words of people very well. It could have been that his age, raging emotions and then adding the death of this father into the landscape, did not help matters.

People would make statements like this, "God needed your father in heaven, more than you needed him on this earth."

Austin would refute that statement to his Uncle Cody. "God is God, He is everything, He is Sovereign, but I am not, and I need my dad!"

They would cry together and then pray and Cody would be in hope that the words of comfort would help the emptiness in Austin. At times it would help, then at other times, Austin would just walk away.

Another statement that would be made by people is, "This was the will of God, this was his time."

Austin would again respond to that in his pain, "It is the Will of God that we are abandoned and left without a dad. If that is God's Will, then God's Will stinks."

It would be an honest and broken moment, yet frustrating for all the Anderson family.

The Anderson's had developed a foundation of faith. The Word of God being the foundation for all things in this life. But now the words of people were challenging the pain in their heart and theology of their faith. It is true that the Bible says in Job 7, *"is there not an appointed time for man on the earth?"* Psalm 90 says, *"The days of our lives are 70 years."* James 4 says, *"Life is but a vapor here today and vanished tomorrow."* Our theology gives us a foundation to place our faith and that is critical. One thing is certain, we will all die. We are not in charge of how we come into this life and we will not be in charge of how we exit.

Jesus handled His departing in the Gospel of John 14 by saying, *"Don't let your heart be troubled..."* This word "troubled" is the word "confused." Jesus is saying, "Don't be confused about what is about to happen. I go to prepare a place for you. I will give you help by sending the Comforter to you." That chapter of John 14 goes on to say, *"He will give us a peace that the world cannot take away."* We cannot explain accidents or deaths that are premature. We cannot explain why some will walk away from accidents and others will not. We cannot explain why little children are taken from us as infants. We just don't know how to explain it, because we are not God. When we understand heaven and we understand how eternity embraces the temporal of this world and our lives, then we are living in understanding that God has us all. Heaven is waiting on us, not our theology.

People would come and say that the devil struck at the heart of the ministry to take Monte out. Over and over again there would be statements made that caused an anger to rise in Austin and Aubrey, a confusion to set in on Allie's heart and Mary's pain. The entire Anderson family was shaken and the words that brought healing were not words of figuring out death, but words that Jesus used: Look to eternity, don't be troubled, this is just for a moment. The Holy Spirit is there to comfort you, and a peace that you cannot comprehend, the Lord will give it to you.

The family walks into the funeral home to see Monte for the first time since that painful night of the accident. It is another moment of finality. This is a very hard moment for the family. The cries of hearts that are broken is evident in the room. The longing that is in Mary's voice, the hardness in Austin's gazing at his dad and the confusion in Allie's young eyes. The brokenness in Don and Carrol is evident. The search for clarity is resonating in the heart of Cody and the rest of the family. There is a movement that draws the attention of everyone in the room. Aubrey rolls his wheel chair back from the coffin. He grips the wheels of the wheelchair and quickly moves himself out of the room. He makes his way outside of the funeral home.

"This is my fault," Aubrey says. "If dad had not came to my game, if we had not stopped to get me something to eat, we would have missed the wreck."

These were torturing words echoing in Aubrey's heart and mind. He was convincing himself that it was all his fault.

There are two voices during crisis. The voice of accusation or the voice of love. God is love! That is who He is. No one can change that, and there is not one course of action in this world that can change who He is. The Bible clearly defines who the voice of accusation is. That voice is the voice of satan. It is the voice of hell. In every accident there will be a shouting voice. These words were driving deeper than the words of people and theology. These words of accusation were tearing apart the faith and the trust that Aubrey had in God.

What voice do you listen to? What are you looking for in the midst of life's challenges? The words of people can help, or they can bring confusion. The words of satan can damage your view of life. In this moment, sitting outside a funeral home that was holding Aubrey's dad and a family that was full of pain, sits a young man in a wheel chair trying to cope. With all that had just unfolded, why was he still on this earth drawing breath, listening to unwanted words. Words, that are actually developing a view of life that would open a door to despair.

Austin was still inside and amid trying to be strong, he was developing a hardness around his heart. "I am mad, I am mad!" He would repeat over and over again. Again, there was words that not only people had said, but that of the enemy at work hardening the heart of a young man. Unwanted words are not only those that are physically spoken in times of tragedy, but the words that satan will choose to plant as a seed in the thought life of the ones walking through crisis. You see, God thrives in faith and the enemy will thrive in fear. When we are in fear, and when we are shaken and scared of the unknown, our heart is open for almost anything. The enemy will take advantage of our weakness. God will cause us to be strong in our weakness. The battle rages in the hearts of these two young Anderson men.

What unwanted words are being spoken to your heart as you read this book? What has unfolded in your life? What circumstances have entered your life that was not expected? Stop allowing the wrong words and the wrong thought patterns to develop in your life. Stop listening to the wrong words of people. Please, stop listening to the wrong thought patterns of the enemy. If you don't stop, then the pattern of your thinking will establish your next steps. Make sure the steps you are taking are founded in God's love. Words can heal, or words can divide. I promise you, when you respond to your circumstance by the word of God's promises and not the enemies lies, you will open your life to healing and restoration. If you allow the words of the enemy to frame your next steps, you will find yourself in the place of despair and emptiness. The Anderson story reveals the reality of that very truth.

Out of the Ashes *Chapter 6* – Finding Refuge

There were over two thousand people in attendance at Monte's funeral. The funeral service itself was testimony to the impact Pastor Monte Anderson had on the lives of people. The service was full of life and celebration, such honor was given to Monte. Mary, the children and the entire Anderson family was ministered to and encouraged from the testimonies and words that were spoken. The funeral procession to the cemetery stretched for miles. It was touching to see a wave of people come and share their condolences. It would not be long however, for the sound of conversation to cease, and the blanket of silence to force its way in as everyone sat at Don and Carrol's house wondering what the next step would be.

The next day Cody went with Mary and the kids to their home. Monte was in the middle of completing some remodel projects. These undone projects literally felt like everything was undone in the natural. Honestly, very reflective of how Mary and the children felt, undone and not complete. Cody made the suggestion that he could find help to complete the projects and, until they were completed, they could stay with Don and Carrol. It was a sense of relief to Mary. She needed people to be close.

Mary thrived around people. Because she loved people, it would be nothing for her to invite someone over last minute or decide to just spend time with someone and say come over. It was a sense of security for her, but also Mary had a gift for talking with people and getting them to open up to where she could minister to their heart. In this moment it was a time for security and help from those that loved her deeply.

The Anderson family has always been very close, and this was a time in which family would surround and help one another. A husband was gone, a father was absent, a son has been taken and a brother is no longer there. Everyone needed a place of refuge and now that place was in the Anderson home. Over the years when people would come to the Anderson home, they would always testify of the peace that was present. Not everything was perfect, and at times that peace would be challenged. But a family who handles their problems on their knees in prayer, is a family that builds a home that holds an atmosphere of peace.

Jesus himself said in John's Gospel, *"The peace I give is a peace that world cannot take away from you."* Peace comes from only one place: God. We think we can find it and replicate it through substance, through people, but the truth is this: True peace only comes by God through the work of His precious Holy Spirit. If God gives, the world cannot take it away. Sure, it can try, but it can't. Peace is like a blanket that covers you when you are cold. There is nothing better than a nice warm blanket that covers you and makes you warm. It can be as cold as a winter day, but I can find warmth if you give me a thick blanket. The peace of God covers you and surrounds you. As you allow that peace to come and fill your life, it becomes tangible and noticeable in your senses. You will sigh with a deep sigh. You may even cry as the warmth of God's peace surrounds you. It is notable, and it is tangible. Allow the Peace of God overflow in your life. Ask for Peace today and I promise that God will respond by His Holy Spirit. Let it come, and let it flow into your life and into your most difficult circumstances.

Austin loved being with his Papa. Don loves his children and grandchildren with all he has. Though he carries strength about him, Don is also one that is revered. Most of those who are close to the family refer to him as the "Duke." Those of you who know John Wayne, then you know what we are saying. Don is resilient, strong, hard-working, and not one who will back down from a challenge. Austin and Aubrey both looked up to Don all their life, especially now in the absence their father. Austin loved to work for his Papa. Austin, in dealing with loss, would look for work. Don, in an attempt to help Austin, would have him help with cattle and farming. Austin, being a strong young man was able to work like three men. As long as he was busy doing something, it would keep his mind off what was happening to his family. There was a role to be fulfilled, and as the oldest son, there was a sense of responsibility that was way too much for a fifteen-year-old boy to place on his shoulders. Austin was strong, and he was strong for his mother and brother and sister.

Aubrey required a lot of assistance for six weeks following the accident. He was uncomfortable and tired of being rolled around in a wheel chair. He would sleep in the living room recliner and then would shift to the couch. If you would have happened to walk into the living room in the morning you would find Mary at the foot of the recliner or at the end the couch for the first week following the accident. She wanted to make sure that Aubrey had what he needed.

Aubrey was the first to ask if they could stay longer at Annie and Papa's house. It was truly a place where he could find refuge from the fear of going home where the absence of his father would be too much to bear at this time. You could tell that he found a comfort in knowing that there was plenty of help around for them. Aubrey had become very quiet. The only thing that was exciting to him was looking forward to playing basketball with his teammates in a few more weeks.

Allie, all of five years old, and quiet, and would find papa's open lap, and crawl up to watch television, and sometimes fall asleep. You could see Mary across the room look and see Allie and know that for this moment, Allie was getting something that was so desperately needed without Monte being here. Allie was Monte's girl. He was so proud to have a daughter, and like most daughters, she had Monte wrapped around her finger. Allie would need the love of a father in her life, and papa would do everything he could to help make up for what was missing in Allie's life.

There were so many times that Mary would try to be strong for the children. That is truly a great attribute in Mary Anderson. Her strength and tenacity had always served her well. Now, without Monte to be strong with her and for her, she felt vulnerable, empty, and alone, even though there were people around. In moments of grief you could hear Mary crying at night when everyone was asleep. With what had just taken place, the truth was that not everyone could sleep very well at all. So as people walked by the bedroom door, you could hear this mother of three so broken and full of grief that words were not enough, and hugs just will not fully fill the void. There were many nights that Austin, Allie, and Aubrey would climb into bed with Mary and they would fall asleep in one bed.

Don and Carrol's house was always like home. The majority of Sunday's would be spent eating lunch after church. Multiple times a week Monte, Mary and the children would be at this house. It was full, and it had life in it. That is why this house of Don and Carrol Anderson had become a refuge, and for a life-giving source for their family to begin a journey of healing. In this journey of grief, we cannot walk through it alone. There must be others to help walk it out. The Anderson's built a place of refuge for support, comfort and strength to help everyone deal with the reality of fearing of the unknown.

We will all run into a form of refuge. For some it will be a substance of some kind. For others that refuge can be our work. For some they will never find a refuge because they just don't know what to do. For Mary and the kids, this was a difficult new reality that they were facing, and the Anderson home was a place of refuge.

Out of the Ashes *Chapter 7* - New Isn't Everything

Just a few miles outside of Ringwood, Oklahoma laid 160 acres of land co-owned by the Anderson brothers. Monte and Cody purchased the land, complete with over 50 acres of fresh timber and wheat fields as far as the eye could see. The initial dream was to sell off some of the timbered property into acreages for home development. Given the new situation that the Anderson family found themselves living out, it only made sense to utilize this location as the new site for them to "press reset" and build a home. Monte and Mary had often discussed this as being a potential plan.

At this point it was unimaginable to go back to the prior house with too many memories filled with the reality that each family member was not yet equipped to deal with. So, with the counsel and support of the rest of the Anderson tribe, Mary picked the top of the tree surrounded hill as the spot to build. It would require creating a much longer than usual driveway to gain access from the adjacent highway, but given how secluded and peaceful the site was, it was worth the work. Mary's intent was to provide a new surrounding for her family. The hope was that this home was to host new memories, establish stability, and restore strength and courage. Underlying the surface of hope, was the concern and reality that not everything new can replace what is missing.

No one ever expected that Monte's life here on earth would be cut short, but if there was one thing that he did well, it was to plan ahead. This, thankfully, was the case when it came to his family's financial future. His foresight laid a foundation of security to build off of in the event of his absence. The house was the first step in this building process. Cody was a valuable resource to Mary as decisions would need to be made concerning the construction of the new home. A close family friend who was brought on as the General Contractor for the project, hired elder brother, Austin, to aid in any and all elements he had the ability to do, or learn along the way. It was of utmost importance to Austin that he be involved in this process. He was no stranger to rolling up his sleeves and putting in hard work. It gave him a sense of purpose to know that, in at least this way, his hands were of those physically responsible in rebuilding the lives of his mother, brother and sister. With that in mind, he poured his heart into every project. From pouring and finishing concrete to roofing, Austin's strength and dedication had touched practically every square foot of the new house. After much work, the home was ready to be occupied. Its newness sparkled with invitation, awaiting the arrival of the Anderson family. Potential to attain the security that had been lost was within reach. Running to something rather than from something seemed a refreshing notion.

From the outside perspective, it appeared that the pieces were starting to come back together, but internally, to those it most effected, Monte's death was still an unresolved issue. While construction of the new house was wrapping up, the sale of the old home was finalizing. One structure, empty of history and a story, yet full of potential: the other, full of memories and love, yet full of anguish from what was now missing. How can these two things conflict any more than this? It seemed to be the theme for everyone surrounding Monte's close circle. The kids, though trying their best to deal, were still noticeably out of sync, but none more conflicted by all this than Mary. She, after all, was the love of his life. Her hope was that this would be the fresh, new thing they needed, and they were all definitely ready for that.

Day by day, week after week, for over a year, they would wake up in Papa's and Annie's home. Austin, Aubrey, and Allie would get ready for school while Mary would prepare herself for anything, she could find to keep her busy. Her days would be spent assisting at the church or helping out with any projects on the ranch. From feeding cattle to driving tractors, Mary was doing her best to drown out the emptiness of grief with the busyness of work. No matter how much she did, it was never enough to bring her peace. Perhaps, she thought, if she could get this house complete and get everyone into the "new", it would bring that peace. She wondered if it was possible. After so much pain, could stability be restored? Can a sense of purpose ever be felt again or is the void just too big? These thoughts are what kept her from sitting still for too long. Even though her finances were secure from not only Monte's management and preparation, but also Cody and the Eldership of Faith Center's decision to continue paying a portion of Monte's salary to the family, Mary needed to be active. Sitting still only reverberated the echo of the seemingly growing void in her heart and mind. Even when surrounded with busyness, there still seemed to be a distant countenance that set in upon her face. During this time, it was on a daily basis that Mary would become emotionally overwhelmed and break into tears.

Anyone who has dealt with loss can attest to the fact that recovery and restoration is a process. The initial step of this process is acceptance. Acceptance of loss is hard because it forces us to deal with the emotions that come along with loss. These emotions always surface questions. A lot of times in the Christian community, we mistake asking God "Why?", with a lack of faith. It is easy to tell someone from afar to trust God and believe that He is able to make everything work out for good, but it is always harder to be the one that receives those instructions.

Mary was in that position. Having been a pastor's wife in a smaller community for so long, she had to feel (whether a perceived reality or not) a sense of pressure to "do the right thing". She was no stranger to taking the role of being the example rather than the exception. In ministry leaders are always on display as an example. Both the good and even the bad will always be on display. There are times that there should be an exception. Death is one of those moments that people should be given the exception. Mankind never plans on dealing with facing the death of a loved one. Thousands of people find themselves facing this very thing every day.

God's original plan was that man would live forever. It was the fall of man in the Garden of Eden that Adam and Eve was tempted by Satan's plan to steal, kill and destroy. That moment in history introduced the concept of death into the earth. Since that time, we have had to go through seasons of dealing emotionally with the loss of loved ones.   This causes us to question God.

Mary's questions were not of God's existence, she was solid in her faith, but rather of His purpose during this season. How could one be expected to rejoice for Monte's gaining of a heavenly home while dealing with his absence in their physical home. Anyone who has dealt with loss can understand Mary's feelings. It is the process of allowing yourself to feel yet continuing to move forward and not let grief become your identity. What a tricky, emotional season.

Healing cannot happen without walking through the emotions of loss, yet if we allow it to, grief will take over and paralyze us. Once grief becomes our identity it quickly takes control of every thought and action. Like a poison released into the bloodstream, there is no part of us unaffected. This is why the Apostle Paul instructed the church in Thessalonica, *"Do not be ignorant concerning those who have fallen asleep and grieve like those who have no hope"* (Thessalonians 4 NKJ). He went on to build a powerful picture of the resurrection of the dead and the coming of the Lord. At some point in our future, we will be reunited once again. One of the primary differences between grief and faith is this: Grief causes one to focus on the present, while faith looks toward the future. This is why most people don't live a faith filled life. Against the desire of the flesh, faith requires you to look beyond the current situation.

Mary was in that place of having to accept the reality of the current yet push beyond to the hope of the future. Only someone who is committed to living by faith understands that challenge. Most people just give up and stay bound by grief, allowing it to become their identity.

While Mary made every effort to push forward, grief was surely attempting to hold her down. Those closest to her watched, much like watching a boxer in the ring fight. We can all shout the right things to do, but the reality is, she was the one absorbing the punches, she was the one having to fight back, and fight back she did. From outside of the ring, voices would shout. Some encouraging, some in opposition, everyone has their own way that they say they would fight if they were in the ring. The problem is, with the most of us, human nature takes over and we just follow the advice of whatever voice is screaming the loudest. We embrace the advice of a coach that may not even be on our side. Grief is the voice that screams the loudest externally during seasons of loss. That is why we must listen from within, to the still small voice during a raging storm of life. This is what gives us the victory.

Mary was visibly being hit hard, but God's voice was speaking to her...and in her own way, she was striking back at this attack on her family. Along with her fight came the emotional ups and downs. Just as spoken of when Jesus found his disciples sleeping after being given specific instructions to stay up and pray, "the spirit is willing, but the flesh is weak." There are moments that Mary would find herself weakened by the toll this journey was taking on her. And this, to all who were close, was more than understandable. God was showing Himself true as the cloud of confusion attempting to move in on her. Mary would hold fast to the Word planted deep in her heart. Everyone was doing their best to be a support for each other as the hope for a new season arose.

When moving time came, the kids were filled with a sense of excitement. In their new home, Austin, Aubrey and Allie were set up far beyond what they had ever experienced in terms of their own space. The entire second story was assigned to the boys. It was complete with 2 bedrooms, 1 bathroom, and even an extra bonus room.

Austin equipped it with such a large sound system that it would shake the entire house. Aubrey's room, not to be outdone by the sound system his brother built in the bonus room, was filled with the latest and greatest gaming equipment on the market. Allie was more than happy to have her room downstairs away from her brothers. It just seemed safer down there, and most definitely fresher in aroma, after all, they were teenage boys. Her private bathroom made the set up complete.

On one hand, this seemed like the perfect layout for the family of four, but on the other hand, it may have been just a bit much for them to take in. The last year of their lives were spent sharing everything while living in Papa and Annie's house. With all this space came the opportunity to disconnect from each other, to compartmentalize away from everyone and everything. While "new" may be exciting, it also opens up unforeseen avenues to the negative potential.

A new school year was at hand. Austin, starting his junior year, Aubrey merging into 8th grade, and little Allie becoming a 1st grader.

"New" surrounded this family of four. New classes, new house, new vehicles, all the things that, from the outside perspective, seemed to be enough to produce an exciting way to move forward. But even with all this newness and the support of a strong family and good church, despair slowly took its toll.

The unfolding of grief echoed the pain that continued to shout loudly from the inside. Sundays would find Mary faithfully attending the church that she and Monte poured their lives into. Her heart was to help fulfill the vision that they started and planted into others. As her and the children would be present in worship, all would do their best to genuinely engage. But at times, you could see the inward struggle surface outwardly. There were moments that it would prove almost impossible to build courage while faith was seemingly crumbling on the inside.

It has been said that the only people who can truly understand the feeling of loss are those who experienced it. And while all nod in agreement with the statement, only those who know can empathetically absorb this statement. The Anderson's were now of those who know. No words deep enough, no action big enough, no effort impactful was enough to fill the void. Grief seems inviting. It is this same grief that will draw you in, masked with understanding, that, if not confronted, will eventually produce a callousness that evolves into anger. That anger will find its way to the surface. Make no mistake, it will take control of our thoughts and responses at such a rapid pace, that others can define it as bi-polar from who we once were.

It's hard to say which Anderson was fighting this more. Allie's young age seemed to isolate her with a bit more innocence. That innocence would be challenged as she watched her mother and brothers process feelings of loss in their own individual ways. Just as it does with any child watching their parents, elder siblings or a leader in life, these actions would frame her future mindset.

"We can make it," Mary would declare to the kids. This was the attitude she wanted them to have about life. Her effort would pay off as that overcoming spirit would show through them in future challenges they faced. Though a sincere effort to build confidence in them, her words would not always match her feelings. There was still a vacancy… an emptiness. And even in a season surrounded by new, the realization was making itself known: just because things are new, doesn't mean all is well.

As the feelings of vacancy played out, Aubrey would find himself on the receiving end. As nature does, the battle for Alpha male began to ensue between older brother, Austin and himself. There is something in the male species that, at minimum, yearns to be respected. This natural tendency, mixed with the testosterone hormonal imbalance of adolescence, caused a battle for power among the two, each striving to find their rightful position while dealing with individual struggles.

Aubrey's, the building presence of guilt from feeling partially responsible for the accident that took his father's life. And Austin's, the inability to go back and have one last moment with dad.

As with any family, having two male siblings in the house always introduces a power struggle. Austin, being the oldest, assumed the role of leader. He was, whether intentionally knowing or not, attempting to fill the perceived missing element, the "man of the house." He felt that someone had to step in as the leader and the decision maker.

It seemed that no matter how much others helped and filled various gaps, it was never quite enough to Austin. Although it could not be defined, there was something Austin was looking for his mother to be. In his mind, no matter how much she disciplined, planned, cooked and tried during this season, to him, it always fell just a tad bit short of the goal. Frustration caused him to place unrealistic demands on Aubrey as well. When pushed too far, Aubrey would reject his guidance as it came across as trying to replace dad. There were more than a few times that Aubrey would just not be in the mood for this. A division was forming in the area of respect.

The irony is, respect was the only reason each one of them were pushing so hard. It seemed, for at least now, that their goal was not being reached. All that being said, there was still the camaraderie of brotherhood among them. They may have fought each other personally, but no one else had permission to do so. They would quickly rise to stand up for each other when faced with external obstacles. "I have your back" was more than just a saying between these two hard headed brothers. That fact would remain throughout their future, but it was the present that challenged them the most. It didn't take long for the small things to escalate into large events.

That is how issues of division work. At first, they seem small, so we just continue to move forward and try to ignore the irritation. But eventually, that small thing, such as a pebble of gravel inside a shoe, causes us so much discomfort that we stop the entire journey. Make no mistake, small things are never small when not dealt with properly and immediately. The pebbles of their situation were causing small things to become mountains of unhappiness, unfulfillment and confusion. It was getting hard to continue the journey. The Anderson's found themselves unhappy yet trying desperately to find moments of laughter. Surrounded by newness, but still unfulfilled.

Lack of fulfillment caused by grief gives anger permission to enter the door of our emotions, resulting in pain. This pain cuts deep and leaves a mark of distrust. This family of four is starting to face the difficult vacant reality of anger as it drives division between them.

It is possible to have determination and faith that God will bring healing yet still avoid personally dealing with the grief of a hurtful situation. Not confronting and talking through things only buries the issue deeper. It never produces the healing to move forward in a healthy way. The wounded spirit has a natural protective tendency to close up and resist the embrace of those that love us the most.

Sometimes the simplest prayer is the most effective. In seasons like this, with layers of internal hurt building one upon the other, the only way to start the healing process is looking to God with one word, "Help". If we can pull ourselves back to the first step, we can deal with, not just the symptoms of the problem, but the root of it as well. There is a reason that the scripture stating "You shall know the truth and the truth shall set you free" rings so powerfully. It acknowledges that the path to freedom is the knowledge of truth. Our issue seems to be that we would rather avoid the truth. But avoiding the truth always proves ineffective. It is only when we identify the truth that we see the reason for our anger in a situation. It is then that we can openly and honestly go to God and admit that we are not able to take this on our own. It is His power and guidance we need to navigate beyond unresolved internal anger. Individually, the Anderson's were angry, but they just weren't sure how to pin point why, and at whom. This anger continued to build walls of isolation between them. The efforts to fill the vacancy by surrounding themselves with "new", didn't seem to be working.

Mary is angry that she is alone. This is hard for her to address because she is surrounded by her kids, extended family and church friends, yet her feelings are still that of a person who has been abandoned. Austin is angry that he now has to live without a dad. Everything he has placed his trust in is now being challenged, and that leaves him in a state of confusion. Aubrey is angry for many of the same reasons. His feelings are very similar to Austin's, yet with the additional layer of an unresolved feeling of blame and guilt. Allie, young enough to not completely understand the entirety of the situation, sees conflicting moments. Some moments of happiness followed by those of hurt. The message she receives is contradicting itself. The people she is looking to for support have yet to find the stability they need to be the pillar she needs in her life. The new material items were not enough to resolve the building anger.

If it is truth that sets us free, as the Bible indicates, then how do we find that truth? How do we identify what is causing us to be angry, so we can stop feeding the grief? According to the Jesus' teachings, it is only in following the leading of the Holy Spirit that one can be led to the truth. The Holy Spirit's function or job, if you will, is to lead us, guide us and direct us. Not only that, the Holy Spirit also comforts us. This is vital in that, sometimes, many times, the direction we are led in exposes us to truths that we will need a supernatural power to cloak us with comfort in order to get through. If we look at God's answers as the truth, then we can also look at grief as the blinder. As long as we embrace the grief, we blind ourselves from the truth.

This is why it is important to be surrounded by people who will help us see God's Word. It feels so natural to run to the anger and grief, but when we realize that they are nothing more than emotional prisons binding us up, we then see the truth: the truth that invites you to exit that prison cell and enter the doorway of truth. To enter the house filled with rooms of restoration. Some, it seems, receive the immediate recovery. While for others, each room holds a bit more of the puzzle pieces needed to restore the image of completion.

No matter how long the process may be, truth is the avenue to freedom. Each one of the Anderson's had to journey down this avenue of truth. They all did it at different times and in different ways. They all would eventually find the healing they needed. It would take time, as it always does. It would be hard and painful, as it often is. Every week would go by and they would continue to give their all-in worship at church. They would volunteer to serve in different areas of ministry as they grew and loved on each other. These would be the things they needed to sustain them as the truth would set in that, being surrounded by new, didn't make things better. The truth was revealing itself, slowly setting them free from the anger and grief, as they allowed it to.

Little did they know, truth was not only trying free them from the current but prepare them for the future. A future that would unfold another devastating tragedy. This, seeming like the end, was only the beginning of the Anderson story.

There is not one Anderson family member that can keep track of the number of athletic events that have been attended over the years in support of one another. Whether it be football, basketball, baseball, softball, or track, this family shows up in full force to show support. Especially since Monte was gone, it was important for Papa, Annie, Cody, and Amy to support Austin and Aubrey in any event that they were involved in.

Austin was in a basketball tournament in Cherokee, Oklahoma. Everyone had just settled into his or her seats and the basketball game was underway when Cody's phone went off. The news on the other end of that call would shake this family to the core of their faith once again.

Dedria, the daughter of Don and Carrol, and her husband H.O. Scott lived in east Texas. Dedria was an Occupational Therapist, and H.O. was an investigative officer for the Harrison County Sheriff's Office. Both of them loved what they did. Together they had two incredible children, Whitney and Heston. Whitney, a tall blonde athletic young lady, is fifteen years of age waiting to turn sixteen. Heston possesses his dad's red hair, and at eleven years old worked hard to impress all and prove that he is just as tough as all his older cousins.

H.O. was about to go on duty for the night. There were many times that the sheriff's office would provide security for the local movie theater, and tonight was H.O.'s turn to provide security. Dedria was finishing up one of their children's baseball games. H.O. had called Dedria and told her that since he was working security tonight, to go ahead and bring everyone to the movies. "I will meet you there," H.O. tells Dedria. What Dedria did not know is that those would be the last words in which she heard H.O. say.

Every word spoken to the ones we love matter. How we end a conversation whether it be face to face, a text or on the phone, it is important to say the right thing no matter if we are upset or even angry. We never know if we will ever get words back or if we have said enough. Life is full of surprises, challenges, and tragedy. We do not know when any one of those will unfold themselves in our lives. After this moment, Dedria would long to have more words from H.O.

He left the house on the way to what would seem to be a routine travel as an officer. The truth is that H.O. held a diversity of jobs. He had worked in the oilfield and even some farm work for Papa. After they moved to east Texas he would be in the Oilfield as well. Even though he held this diversity of experience there was a sense of fulfillment for H.O. in the uniform he had the honor of wearing. H.O. grew to truly love serving and protecting people. The patrol car is rolling down the highway that H.O. had traveled countless times. Everything is familiar to him. He continued down a highway that held the scenery of the same trees, the same houses, and the same turn in the road.

Out of nowhere, a deer bounds onto the highway from the ditch. The deer's head made an immediate lunge into the passenger's side front wheel, this causing the vehicle to spin out of control. H.O.'s cruiser turns sideways into the opposite lane on the highway, right in line with a large Dodge pickup coming from the other way. In a sudden moment of time, in a place that is so familiar, the Dodge pickup makes such an impact on H.O.'s patrol car that it burst into flames, there was nothing that H.O. could do to save himself. In a matter of minutes the car is consumed by fire. Because of the impact H.O. has no ability to free himself from the fire. The ammunition in trunk of his patrol car begins to discharge causing anyone attempting to help to take a step back.

This deputy sheriff is consumed by the fire.

Dedria pulled into Walmart before she met H.O. at the movies to pick up some household items. Walmart is the center stop for this community as it is in most small rural areas. Dedria, sees a number of families and friends as she is walking thru the aisles. She see's many people answering their phones. She thought to herself, "Everyone is busy on the phone." What she does not know is that this community of friends are all taking about a friend named H.O. who has just driven for the last time.

Dedria picks up her last item and heads to the check-out lane. As she stands in line, there is a gentleman in the next line over that Dedria knew. He was a brother to a fellow deputy of the sheriff's department. He is on the phone and waves at Dedria. She continues to check out and overhears this gentleman say, "Dedria is right here." On the other end of the phone the voice is telling him that they have been trying to locate Dedria. "Do not let her leave, but don't tell her anything, the Sheriff wants to talk to her first."

He hangs up the phone and begins to walk to Dedria. She has picked up her bags and with the kids they are on their way out. A woman who is a counselor at the children's school walks up to Dedria and with tears in her eyes and compassion in her voice says, "Dedria, I am sorry."

Right then Dedria knew that something had happened and that something had to do with her husband and the father of her children. The gentleman stopped the lady from saying any more and says, "She does not know anything yet".

The optical store was closed at this point and they take Dedria into that closed store with many people in Walmart surrounding the children. This optical store inside Walmart has just became ground zero for a tragedy that has struck a community. This man who just happened to be at Walmart at the same time as Dedria begins to tell her what information he has.

The Sheriff arrives and began to unfold the details of what happened to H.O. Dedria fell to her knees in the middle of this store while everyone begins to watch in dismay.

"Take me there, I want to see him, I want to be with him" Dedria cries out.

The sheriff explains to Dedria that there is nothing to see and it would be to tragic for the children to go and view what is left.

"He is gone," said the sheriff.

That is when Dedria made the call to her brother Cody. Cody answers the phone, his sister Dedria is somewhat calm asking what he was doing. "We are all at Austin's basketball game."

Dedria replied, "I have tried to call dad, but I have not been able to get ahold of him." Then Dedria breaks down and as she is crying, she says, "H.O. has died in an accident tonight."

Cody stands up during this ballgame and moves away from the crowd to a hall way where he can hear better. He could not believe what he is hearing on the other end of the conversation.

"Can you please repeat what you are saying and tell me what has happened?" he asks her again.

"Cody, it has happened again," Dedria cries out.

As Dedria and Cody talk on the phone, they cry together, and Cody assures her that they will get things put together as soon as they can and make their way to where she is. Cody goes back to the crowded game and asks for Amy, Annie and Papa to come out to the hallway of the gymnasium. As the game continued to play, the crowd yelling in support of their team a family that is already broken holds each other and cries more tears of the impossibility that they have been struck again by the uncertainty of death.

The family gets all of the things that they need and make their way in the night to drive eight hours to where Dedria, Whitney and Heston live. While driving through the night Cody looks through the windshield. The suburban that they are driving is full of family that has some asleep but some in shock. The sky that night was clear. The light from the moon and stars illuminated the roadway. As Cody stared into the night his faith is being challenged and the questions are flooding his mind. How could this be happening again? Can this family hold on to their faith and trust in God through another loss?" "How will Dedria and the kids be taken care of, they are so far from us?" "Who will love on them and surround them?"

Cody had watched the support flood into Mary and children and knew that it would be critical for Dedria and her children. Then the difficult question begins to surface in his thoughts. God, where are you? That question was very frustrating because as a Pastor, Cody had responded to that question from those in whom he had ministered to countless times. On this night, this long drive to his sister's home, and her children wrestling with what has just taken place, everyone in the Anderson family is confused.

Back in east Texas, the Sherriff has escorted Dedria, Whitney, and Heston to their home. Dedria's house was located off a small Texas highway. When they turned off the highway, the mile-long blacktop road was filled with cars from concerned people in the community. There were over 100 people waiting for her to arrive to show how much they would miss this servant and friend of the community.

If you want to measure the impact of one's life after they have finished their race on this side of heaven, then you must watch the response after they are gone. H.O. was quiet but strong. He would do anything for anyone, just to be a help. As Dedria drove through all of the cars, she saw that his life had great significance and that he would be dearly missed by this community.

There is a massive amount of confusion that is setting in for Whitney and Heston. Where is my dad and why can't I see him? Whitney's friends have come and upon the family's arrival, they go to her bedroom to be with her. Heston tries to be close to his mother, and as a crowd of people continue to fill his home, he tries to make sense of what has taken place. Actually, what Heston is seeking is not much different from what all the Anderson family would be seeking at this time. Their hearts were beating the same statement: "God our view is being challenged on where you are, and we need help!"

The enemy of our faith is satan. The enemy comes to steal kill and destroy. Many times, we look at the one that has left us and those of faith will rest on this statement: "The enemy has stolen something from us". What we must understand is that the enemy is present in any tragedy to steal any hope and faith in God. You see, the enemy knows that latter part of that oh so powerful verse.

"The enemy comes to steal, kill and destroy, but I have come that you may have life and it more abundantly". (John 10:10 NKJ)

Since creation the enemy has been working against man to blame the Creator for what is wrong. In the Garden of Eden satan succeeded with Adam and Eve when he stole from them, the clear view of who God was to them.

"you can be just like God and see all that he sees if you will just take a bite of this fruit from the tree of the knowledge of good and evil" satan said to Eve, when God had told them, "of everything in the garden you can take of, but not this one tree."

The enemy succeeded in building a vision in Adam and Eve that was opposite of what God had intended for them. Because he succeeded in that effort, he stole their view of God. When that view of God was absent it was easy to turn on what God had told them not only to do, but who He is to them.

In the midst of tragedy, the enemy comes to steal our view and opinion of God so that we will question where God is. If the enemy can steal the correct view of God, then he can rob us of faith and trust in the only one that brings healing and restoration in the midst of such desperation and loss. The Anderson family is reeling with the reality of what is truly being stolen. A faith and trust in God who holds the bigger picture that is larger than one person. Cody gripped the steering wheel a little tighter and with tears welling up in his eyes the questions continue to flood in.

The family pulled into the driveway at Dedria's home at daybreak. The scene is all too familiar. Everyone embraces one another. The sobbing and crying are unbearable, and the pain is very deep. Over and over again you hear the statement being made by this family to one another, "Not again, no! No! not again!"

The look of despair on Dedria's face was enough to sink anyone. The confusion in the eyes of Whitney and Heston would bring anyone to a place of asking questions. "How can this dad be gone?" "Who is going to be there for them?" "How will they step through the things of life without that strong presence of H.O. being with them?"

H.O. was a strong man with a large heart of protection. Carrying that heart forward, Dedria begins the first day without him determining that, as a family they will be strong. This is where faith begins to work for each us. What Dedria begins to do is place her faith in the strength of God. The Word of God tells us that when we are weak, He is strong. There is a strength to be found, and that strength requires faith. On many occasions, Dedria would remind herself of Job. The declaration of her heart was that if God could restore the character Job in the Bible, then God could begin to restore to her what was lost. She had walked a journey by watching what we had just went through with Monte just months prior to this moment. That journey still being traveled, taught Dedria that Heaven always wins in the end for each of us. For Monte's life, who is now in heaven, caused Monte to win. Because her brother Monte, that is rejoicing in heaven right now, he has gained victory over death. She sees Monte and the victory that he has gained.   Now, she can make this same journey with her husband being gone.

There was a fight in the depths of Dedria. As a woman driven by faith, what do you do with this loss? She determined that heaven is gaining and if heaven has gained, God will not leave her without. Wow! That is faith in action. A determination that H.O. was heavens gain and, though it was an incredible loss for this family, no doubt about that. H.O. gained everything that day. Stepping into the presence of the Lord for eternity what an incredible place of faith.

Dedria would continue to build that picture in the heart of her children that even in our hurt and loss, daddy has gained everything. The morning before the funeral service Dedria talks with Whitney and Heston.

She loves on them and tells them, "We are going to be strong today. Do we really believe in God? This is our test to our faith and understanding that God is at work in the midst of all this."

Whitney and Heston agree to be strong but on the inside the two of them are fighting many warring thoughts. Why? Why my dad? Why us?

Tragedy will never give us the answer. "Why?" We make every attempt to get that question answered and we need to stop. Cody was asked by Dedria to do the service. There were other family members involved and it was a beautiful service of honor. In the service Cody began to share the testimony of loss that this family has just walked through and now with H.O.'s family, here we are.

Cody then makes a statement, "Why is the grass green, and why is the sky blue?" He continues, "Why did God create all He did? We will not know the answer to why grass is green and the sky blue, what we do know is that God was and is continually at work in the midst of it."

When we can stop asking the question "Why" and turn that into, "What is next?" Then we can begin see differently. There is still life to be lived, children to be raised and purpose to be fulfilled. Dedria held onto that foundation. It does not move us forward when we stay in the land of "Why." Let's focus on what is next. This initial step of Faith in action brought strength to Dedria as she led her family forward towards healing.

In the midst of the service Pastor Cody asked for every head to bow and eye to close. He talked about the greatest testimony of H.O.'s life was not what he did for the community, as an investigator for the Harrison County Sheriff's Department, as dad or as husband, but that He has accepted the love and forgiveness of a Savior, Jesus Christ.

Today if you are shaken to the core of your own mortality, that if you draw your last breath on this earth forever, you will meet God in whom created you. Are you ready? Are you prepared?

In that moment, waiting to respond was H.O.'s father Herman and a brother-in-law Arthur. They indicated that day they were in need of a Savior and accepted Christ as their Lord.

God can use the ashes of a man's testimony and tragedy to capture the heart of a man without a Savior. Dedria and all the Anderson family, that day they saw that God was actively at work in their midst. From Heaven's view, H.O. would pay any price to see a family member know Christ and the Salvation of our God. Was that in God's sovereign plan for H.O. to pay such a price for the salvation message to come to a family members heart? We don't know, but what we do know is that for the family, we know that our God is always at work in the midst of tragedy.

At the graveside the number of police, highway patrol and emergency workers were all over one mile long. Hundreds of friends and family came to the graveside. The police guard honoring H.O. and presenting Dedria with a State of Texas flag was one of the most moving moments. A front-page article shows this strong woman of Faith sitting by her father and this father, Don Anderson has his arm around her as the police fire off their shots in honor of the fallen. That arm is more than a picture for the front page of a newspaper. It is a picture of a Heavenly Father wrapping His arm around one of His own and providing the strength that Dedria has exhibited the faith to walk in.

Months would follow and Dedria would take a folding chair along with her lunch and would drive to that cemetery still exercising her faith with a strength that was not her own. That strength would build with each visit. She would have a conversation with H.O. She would tell him what she was doing in the week and what had happened with the kids. She knew that heaven was watching, and that heaven was providing strength for her sorrow. Each time that she would do it, a greater sense of peace would come, and healing began to be evident to her heart.

Breaking through grief is more than just saying "I want to." It is taking the step of faith, to add strength to your life. As humans, we are very guilty of trying to shut everything out and everyone away from our pain. When we decide that our strength is not enough and know that God is at work in every situation, then we are taking a solid step of faith to gain the strength that He has for us.

Is it really that easy? Let's ask a question: How easy is it to bring light into a dark room? Just turn on the switch and that switch will send a signal to a power that we do not have on our own. Flip the switch and the power goes to the light and it is revealed. Grief and sorrow will ask you to keep the light off. When you turn the switch on you are releasing a power that is not even yours but God's. It works, and it is that easy. It must be done every day of our lives when we are going through loss. Turn on the switch, take the step of faith to begin adding strength. Over time grief will not be holding your view of who God is, but faith will arise, and you will have the strength to trust that God is still at work in your life and all can be restored.

"How you view life will be determined by what has framed your current state of mind." This is the common denominator, which ironically creates and defines how we each can take away differing opinions when viewing the exact same thing. Some walk-through life seeing a cloudy day as gloomy and depressing while others may see it as hopeful due to their understanding of the need for rain. When we look out at the world around us, we view it through the prism our experiences have framed. It is a natural tendency to use the information given to us through the filter of this prism to help us determine the response we should have for each situation. After all, the prism has been formed personally by our own lives.

This is why some people have a less than positive response to certain things while others may have a more uplifting, hopeful outlook. Difficulty, pain, and hardship of the past have formed a prism in some lives that only allow things to be seen and viewed through that perspective. The same goes for the opposite. One may see a joyous potential, simply because their past experience has been one of that very thing. What would it be like if we could change that prism? What would happen if we could adjust the view of how we see the world around us? The good news is, it is very possible.

The prism originally handed to the Anderson family is being greatly challenged and changed by the events of late. Standing in the midst of the ashes are left two wives turned widows at an extremely young age, 2 sets of children left fatherless. And even though each have been handed the same situation of these tragic automobile accidents, they will all be personally taking away different thoughts, views and feelings about the same circumstance.

The Marine Corps seemed to be an obvious fit for Austin. There was no doubt that this young man had a "fight" on the inside of him. If that fact was ever questioned, all you had to do was ask his opposing member of the challenging football team. Once he was assisted back onto his feet, that is. Austin's, athleticism and work ethic were growing to an above average level, it was also becoming evident that there might be some internal issues stirring within. It did not take a lot on certain days to get Austin "fired up" as the family would say. Perhaps it was an internal obligation he felt to provide for himself that drove him, but the downside was a shutting and closing off to loved ones at times. "I just need to get away," is a pretty common term to hear from a young man transitioning into adulthood. But for Austin, it was the anger being filtered through his prism that was driving his feeling of this need to disconnect. While good was at work and surrounding him, it was very hard to see. And for these reasons, after the completion of his first year of college, he joined the military and set out on a new course.

The bottom of a bottle would prove to be the place Aubrey Anderson would end his days in a search for peace and resolve. His joining of the Navy came as no huge surprise as, while in high school, everyone watched him excel in sports. His natural gift with the ability to command a presence when he walked into the room was balanced out by the fact that his quiet demeanor allowed you to see the gentle giant that lived beyond those sparkling blue eyes. Even though he was handed all these assets on the surface, there was a growing hurt beyond. He was unable to shake the feeling of guilt and responsibility connected to his father's accident. It is hard for an 11-year-old to healthily dissect and understand the passing of their parent, especially if the information being processed points towards them anyway. As he grew older, this idea did not pass but instead grew along with him. Eating away at the peaceful moments he would have; this feeling would eventually find its way to the surface and the symptom would result in the presence of an unhealthy habit. Succeeding in sports would not fill it. Succeeding in the military would not fill it. It was a gaping hole infecting a wound that was not going away.

Allie Joy Anderson, being so young when the original tragedy struck their family, is having a hard time processing all the immediate change. As time goes by, the resolve doesn't seem to be surfacing. She watches as the brothers she loves struggle to find themselves. As her mother tries desperately to move forward in the haze of confusion that comes along with the sudden, unexpected loss of a spouse. While family members seem to be cracking at times, spewing out emotion and anger toward each other, she begins the search for her own identity. This search, in many ways would lead her into an unhealthy clinging on to relationships. Being the paradigm shaped by the experience of losing a father at such a young age, it is understandable how this would be the reaction. It would seem that now, in her high school years, this search was not filling the void as she had hoped. Emptiness and loneliness were the voices most loudly speaking in her ears.

Standing there on the basketball court her senior year, Whitney Scott finally starts to break down. Her determination to keep moving forward and prove that she is fine and doesn't need help is over shadowed by the moment she found herself standing mid-court looking at the spot where her dad used to position himself. His absence could not be ignored by her heart, mind and emotions. Long overdue and greatly anticipated, the hurt surfaced from within. Her plan to just not talk about it as treatment for healing was not proving to produce peace or help. She was learning, in this moment, that in life, things don't just go away if we try not to think about them. They have to be dealt with. And Whitney was understandably having a hard time with this.

Having been such a young man when his father passed, Heston Scott was unsure how to deal with it. His continuous desire to just please his dad was not unusual for a young boy. There is something about the presence of a man in a boy's life that makes them want to rise up and gain respect in their eyes. What haunted Heston the most about the sudden absence of his father was the fact that his last encounter with his dad was one of emotion. His heart was angry at his dad due to being disciplined by him that day. Like most of us, the initial response to discipline is not joyful, and for a young man to lose his father during that moment, feelings of guilt and shame, can later result in emotional instability. Time would prove that there would arise moments where Heston would lash out in sports events and at classmates. His desire to go back and change the past could not be fulfilled, so his actions began to make him consumed with controlling the present, even if it was in an aggressive manner. The view he had on life was affecting everything he saw around him.

The caption at the beginning of Psalm 91 declares this before one unfolds verse 1: *"(Safety of abiding in the Presence of God) He who dwells in the secret place of the Most High shall abide under the shadow of the Almighty."*(Psalm 91:1 NKJ)   There is a place of safety for every person under God's creation, it is designed by God.

Now, for those who submit their lives to God as their Heavenly Father, and to the Savior Jesus Christ, and receive the transforming power of the Holy Spirit, there is a promise. The promise that as one submits their life (or abide) with God, He will be their covering. In that covering you will be safe! Without a covering you are exposed to the pain of fighting through the course of this world alone. In Ephesians chapter five the Bible places the man at the head of the home and compares that covering, to Christ as the head of the church. Without Christ at the head of the church, the church falls into the depths of its own desires and becomes powerless. When the covering over a family is missing, those in the family will lose their safety and covering.   They will make any attempt to replace that safety.   The kind of safety where love produces such a high level of security to a home and every person who dwells in that home possesses a sense of security.   Every one of us is created to need a covering.   It is that submission and draw on the heart strings of our life that says there is a power that is higher than I.

In America today, fathers are missing out of the homes of many families. One can look at the troubled youth in America and see that the majority of them do not have a father to influence their life in a positive way. One can also look at the broken young women without a father showing them unconditional love and providing security and safety for them, not only physically but emotionally. These same young women make every attempt to replace that love with those things that are abusive just to get attention. It is not that every home with a father in it will not have struggles and be perfect, that is just not reality. The Word of God builds a foundation for us that releases tremendous power for every home to live under. As a home and the leadership of that home submits its life to the leadership of God's Word and the work of the Holy Spirit

There is a covering that provides a safety and security for a home to thrive in. When that foundational truth is missing from a home, then security and safety is not present.   When it is not present, we are seeking for something to fill that void.

This family, these children without a covering are exposed emotionally and even in the framing of how they think and view the world. Anger, self-pride, emotional instability, confusion, and the list could go on and on. The natural covering of their lives is missing and now comes the pursuit of a Heavenly Father that will never leave them or forsake them.

When we begin to abide under the shadow of the Almighty, we will find safety and security for our lives. Our view of the world will become His view. When pain is healed, the view through our eyes make a shift from the pain of yesterday to the hope of tomorrow. We all seek for a covering, let's just make sure that it is the right covering.

How we view the world we live in, depends on the health of our covering.

It is 2005 and Austin is stationed at Camp Bahrain, Marine Base in Fallujah, Iraq in the Al Anbar Province. There was a man-made lake in the middle of the base, but the military had to place pump stations outside the base in order to get more water into the lake which would then be filtered. The Marine Corp had engineers to work the water stations and generators. Austin was one of those engineers. On this night this marine who was trained and skilled as an engineer would have to draw on his marine combat training in order to survive.

The light from the ringing phone on the bedside table fills the room. Startled, Cody sits straight up and looks at the phone. The number ID on the phone was not familiar.

Cody answers the phone with a groggy voice. "Hello".

"Uncle Cody," said the voice on the other end.   "Are you there, Uncle Cody?"

Cody could tell that it was Austin even though the connection was not the best. Cody replied, "Yes, Austin. How are you?"

"I am doing okay.   Well, that is not true I need prayer for safety, our base is under attack." Austin's voice began to crack, and Cody could tell that something had taken place on the sands of Iraq. "We have been commanded to stand down and take cover.   The enemy is approaching the base with a cache of mortars and rounds are being fired onto the base. I need prayer," Austin said with a stern but broken voice.

All kinds of thoughts were flooding into Cody's imagination as Austin went on to share what was taking place and how he needed to have a peace of mind. Austin's voice became like a sound in the background. As he continued to talk, Cody began to reflect how Austin had arrived at this dangerous point in his life. He would quickly remember how this tall, blonde haired, blue eyed, strapping young man came to him and Papa at the end of this senior year and shared with them that he had been talking with a marine recruiter.   Both of their hearts sunk deep within when Austin shared that he believed it was his desire to become a Marine.   At the same time a sense of pride and patriotism rose within them and they became proud of Austin, which was not hard to do.

Austin is a natural leader.   When Austin walks into a room of people, he stands out.   Not just because he is tall in his stature and a sharp looking young man. He is loud! When he talks, he is the loudest person in the room. When he laughs, he is contagious. Austin is so strong and full of life. He would tackle anything and if one person was to tell him he could not do it, he would figure out a way to pull it off. Austin is perfect for the Marine Corp. So, he graduated high school and stepped into a journey that would define the rest of his life.

After arriving at Camp Pendleton in San Diego, the entire Anderson family steps onto the graduation field to watch Austin.   As he marched by the family, they could not believe their eyes. This strong, larger than life young man had lost over 50 lbs. He was so thin that he looked like he had been in a concentration camp. He literally had zero body fat. He would later share with the family that basic training in the Marine Corp was the most difficult and challenging thing he had ever gone through.   "They broke everything down in me to my lowest point, to the point where I thought I could not do absolutely anything but breathe and that is it" said Austin. He would continue to make this statement over and over, "I may be a part of Marine Corps, but I still hold onto my core, which is God."

Every member of the Anderson family watched Austin, holding back the tears. All could see a young man who had given up everything and had to battle physically to become a strong Marine.

Following basic training, Austin went through engineer training for the Marine Corp, constantly trying to find a sense of direction for his future. He did know one thing for certain. He wanted to be a Marine officer so that he could make a difference, not only in himself, proving that he could do it, but also make a difference in others.

Following his training, he was stationed as a Marine Reserve at Wichita, Kansas. He would attend classes at Oklahoma State University and work his reserve responsibilities one weekend a month.

Austin was becoming a man, making decisions that affected his future.   Becoming a man does not mean that there is not broken places of a teenage boy still trying to find a sense of healing. Austin was staying busy with school and the Marine Corp attempting with all his ability to be successful. Relationships with home were very difficult for Austin. He was not approving of his mother's decisions, and he made that clear to everyone.   Even amid the struggle with Mary, he deeply loved her and would sacrifice anything to help when she needed something. It was never a secret to what Austin was thinking at this time, because the Marine Corps had made this loud personality even more expressive.   There were certain things that he wanted for his sister Allie. Mary had her steps and her plans that needed to be walked out and Austin and Mary did not see things in the same light. Even though they did not agree on very many things, you could still see that they cared for each other.   They possessed a strong bond that would continue to show the strength that Mary and Austin both held onto.

When brokenness stays in the background, it will always be shouting in the foreground of relationships. We cannot in our emotional makeup, filter our responses to circumstances, without going through our brokenness first. When everything filters through brokenness, then that is what we see, brokenness! Honestly, it is a very simple truth that has very large consequences. When a shift comes, and brokenness is brought out to look at and talk about, the healing can begin.

Austin, still broken and Marine strong, was trained to fight, even when you are broken. Get through it! Be strong enough to press through it. While all of that is a true statement, you can never truly get through it, or truly overcome it until the broken places are healed. This was a family still broken and still at war with one another. For Austin, it was easier to stay away and work hard then it was to be close and always arguing with his family.

The phone is silent on the other end when Cody asked Austin, "Can I pray with you?"

Austin said, "That is why I called."

"Before I pray with you, I want to share with you a phone call I received yesterday. Our good friend from Australia called and asked about you, Nigel McNeil. I told him that you were deployed, and he told me that he had been praying for you and that you are protected."

The two talked longer about the timing of that call, which came at the beginning of the officials announcing the imminent attack. A relief came over Austin and they said their good byes. The threat backed down that very day. A clear sense of God's hand of protection over Austin gave him a sense of safety and confidence that God had his back and was not allowing something to be taken from him.

There was a "trust" shift that week in the middle of the sands of Iraq that opened this Marine's eyes to the fact that he was not invincible, but vulnerable. A shift of where he needed the mighty hand of God over his life, because he was not strong enough to protect himself from all the dangers of this world. A shift that caused Austin to no longer trust only in his own ability but trusting in the hand of the Almighty God who loves us and is for us.

God is not working against us but is walking with us. A shift that says in this moment, I need God! Austin, at the center of his brokenness, viewed God as a taker, because of the loss of his father. In a moment this brokenness was brought to the forefront, no longer hiding in the background, and Austin realized in the sands of Iraq, that he needed God and God had proved to him that He was a giver and a protector.

It is not only about needing God but also needing to "trust" God. In the Word of God, it says, *"Trust in the Lord with all your heart and lean not on your own understanding." (Proverbs 3:5 NKJ)* When there are broken things in and around your heart, you will not make that shift.   It is when you surrender the brokenness unto the Lord that a shift happens. A shift that says this: "You will not understand everything that happened, the way it happened and why it happened." "It is okay, I trust you God and you will protect and lead me."

Austin made that step, yet it was when he was under fire and when he was uncertain of what the morning would bring. He said, "I trust you God," and the broken places began to heal and then another began to heal, starting a flow of healing and restoration in his life. It affected not only him, but his family. You could see the change when he returned home.

Returning from Iraq a soldier, Austin was a strong leader in his unit, receiving promotion, and being promoted to Sargent. With a clear look in his eye and a new sense of purpose, he was determined to finish college and pursue a career in the Marine Corps. He sets his eye on Oral Roberts University in Tulsa, Oklahoma. Coming to Oral Roberts had been a dream of Austin's for years. One of the issues facing Austin was the cost of a private university. He was determined and with a powerful "trust" that shifted his life towards God, he was ready to take on the challenge. There was something different about Austin.   A sincere faith was being built in him. A pursuit of God that was genuine. A restoring of relationship between he and his family was becoming evident. He was trying, and it was paying off. He chose to invest not only in his faith and trust in God, but to invest in those whom he loved.

By this time, Mary and Allie had moved to Norman, Oklahoma. There would be many times that he would go and visit, take them to eat and spend time with a now teenage sister that so needed her big brother around. Aubrey had just joined the Navy and the only conversation that would be had would have to take place on the phone. Austin's leadership, his drive and enthusiasm for life would begin to be felt by everyone in his family. Austin was strong and determined and had a large impact on everyone he surrounded.

In 2009 Austin was called up for his second tour to Iraq. With a sense of commanding leadership as Marine Sergeant, and a confidence that God is with him, he serves his country. Things would shift on this deployment, though not as dangerous as the previous one. Austin served on a Military Transitional Team, training Iraqi soldiers. This deployment had moments of danger because the convoys that had to be dispatched into and through the Basra regions. These convoys would work with the nationals as they swept houses and investigated insurgents. Austin created a trading system to improve maintenance efficiency, making work smarter and not harder for the Marines under him.

Austin had a great impact among many young men and women that served with him. If you came to Austin's office you would see two things, his Bible and some form of leadership book. If you were to talk with him, you would get some of both.   Austin became so dedicated to leadership and his Christian faith that he was not bashful to share. As a leader, and officer, he carried a lot of influence.

Austin had begun to take the broken pieces of his life and trust God with them. You may not have been under the fire of Iraqi forces to cause you to look at what you do trust in, but as long as you are drawing breath you can do it. Lay down the broken pieces and simply say, "God I trust you." Can it be that simple? Yes! All the way through this we are challenging you to take the simple steps and watch God begin to heal and restore. Austin shifted everything, and his destiny and his purpose was unfolding before him.

Following this second tour in Iraq, Austin was asked to serve in Washington D.C. They were small deployments, but he had found tremendous favor with Marine Corp leadership. Many saw that Austin was a strong leader and someone who could get the job done. While in Washington D.C. Austin was promoted to Staff Sergeant, as well as the choice to renew or retire from the Marine Corps. This would be a time of difficult decisions.

Cody looks down at his phone that is ringing and sees that it is Austin. "Hello buddy what is going on?" Answered Cody.

"I am working through this decision about my future," said Austin. He continued, "I love what the Marine Corps has done for me, but I believe that God is leading me into building business ideas and concepts to help ministries."

Austin was constantly working on building something better and getting organizations to function at a higher level of efficiency. For Austin everything could be better, bigger and greater than where it currently was. If he was able to figure out a way to do it, and he had the right resources around him, he could get it done.

"I believe that the door is beginning to close on the Marine Corps and that my time has come to serve God at a higher level in building avenues to help grow ministries," Austin exclaimed.

Cody responds, "God has been with you every step you have made, from the Marine Corps to coming to a college that has been virtually taken care of financially, which is a miracle in itself. God has been faithful to you. He will continue to do that, follow what is in your heart and what God is leading you to do."

We need to pause for a moment and highlight something for you. When you shift your trust to God, you have confidence in taking your plans to Him so that they can be molded into His plan and His purpose. God is thinking of you and He is for you!   When you stop just trusting in yourself alone, and begin to trust in God for His protection, and His purpose being done in your life, it produces a confidence in you.   A confidence that says, "God here I am and here is what I see, is this my next step?" That is what Austin was doing and God was leading him into a greater purpose.

During this time, Austin had met a wonderful, beautiful, and smart young woman named Elizabeth Thaxton. It was in the midst of the coffee shop on the ORU campus that the two met. When Elizabeth first met Austin, she thought that he was arrogant. But there was something about this man on campus that was a leader and would steal the attention of any room, and she was drawn to that leadership in spite of his over confidence. She saw something in Austin that drew on her heart. It took several dates before Austin would convince her that he was the real deal, and his arrogance was simply confidence and that she needed him to make her life complete. At least that is the way Austin looked at it.

Truth be told, it was this northern girl from Minnesota that would claim Austin's heart, and their journey would begin right on Oral Roberts University, a place of definition for this Marine, and the unfolding of a future that was world changing in Austin's heart.

Out of the Ashes *Chapter 11* - The Navy Airman

September 1st, 2008, Aubrey Anderson stands at a Naval Air Station in Pensacola, Florida, looking at a very familiar sight from his Oklahoma past. It is not usual for a tornado to make its appearances in the panhandle area of the Gulf Coast, but with the air pressure build up stirring from nearby Hurricane Ike, there it was. The irony of this young man having had a major storm rip through his life's path in a very real way, contrasted with the fact that, being raised in Oklahoma, he had witnessed more than a few handfuls of tornados touch down much too close to his home, was a harsh reminder of the season of life he found himself living. Something about Aubrey standing there watching a violent, raging tornado, was horribly and ironically poetic.

The thing about a tornado is that it develops over places of stillness. Opposing wind currents develop and collide mid-air. When they do, it's the people on the ground, the residents of the quiet, still environments that get hit with the destruction. Nothing could describe Aubrey's life more closely than this. And yet, there he stood. While others ran for places of protection and safety, there was something on the inside of him that was far too familiar, even comfortable with the presence of a raging storm. Though it would settle throughout the night, the fact that it presented itself before him on this day, spoke of something deeper. States away from his past in Oklahoma, there it was at his door.

Once again, the tornado in Aubrey's life continued to spin.

After weeks of training, Aubrey found himself climbing inside a Helo-dunker for training. For the majority of readers who are unaware of what a "Helo-dunker" is, let me save you the research. It is a simulated training which prepares the Naval Aircrew and rescue swimmers for an ocean or water-based helicopter crash.

Aubrey entered the back of the simulator and made his way to his seat. He reached for the 4-point harness and buckled himself in, while three petty officers yell instructions.

"Listen up, this is what you are about to experience. You will be lowered into the water. As soon as you are completely lowered into the water, the simulator will be turned upside down in the water. It is up to you, unharness yourself and find your way out."

Aubrey had watched other groups go before him and he was confident that it would be an easy task. Others had done it, so why not him? (this was the usual mindset in which he operated). As the simulator was lowered into the water, the nerves began to rise, and confidence was fading quickly. It a matter of seconds the entire simulator is submerged and then, in a fast motion, much like in the eye of the tornado, the simulator abruptly turned upside down. Aubrey reached up to the middle of his chest to release the harness holding him in, yet shockingly, nothing will unlock. Aubrey lifts off his mask and signals for the safety diver to come and help. There is a rip cord attached to the seat, which, when pulled, releases the entire harness apart from the seat. The safety diver swims over to pull the rip cord, and upon doing so, nothing was unlocked. Aubrey sat underwater still locked into his seat. Panic began to build, and at this point, Aubrey did not know how much longer he could hold his breath. Aubrey's response to the panic was to allow all the remaining air in his lungs to be released. The last thing he saw was the face of the rescue diver as he blacked out.

Following high school graduation in May of 2006, Aubrey moved to Stillwater, Oklahoma to attend college. Aubrey could not wait to get out of the small town of Ringwood and begin his life away from the persona of being a preacher's kid. He loved to do whatever it took to be the life of the party. Aubrey had come to such a place of unfilled answers in his life that the question marks expanded in his heart. The question marks so consumed who Aubrey was, that he no longer possessed a faith in religion, faith in God, or even a faith in others. After all, he thought his father was a preacher and look what happened to him.

The question mark. What lies behind every moment of tragedy, every moment of loss, is questions.   Every person that is on the backside of these types of moments must walk through the questions and find the answers they need. If the searching for answers linger, the door opens to our imagination to leave what is reality. To walk away from finding the answers that one needs, is like walking through the desert lost looking for water. If you don't find the water to sustain you, the desert will consume you. In the desert there is not life sustaining resources, and when you can't find the answers to the questions of tragedy, nothing you pursue will be able to satisfy you, and that is where Aubrey found himself.

The college party scene consumed Aubrey. At the end of the first semester he all but failed every class. The hangovers became so consistent in Aubrey's life that he simply did not care about his classes. Being left alone to become his own man had brought Aubrey to the place where he had lost his purpose and the desire to pursue higher education. Finally, the call came from Papa.

Don said, "Aubrey there is no sense in paying for school if this is the kind of effort you are going to give!"

Aubrey found himself stuck. He had no idea what he wanted from life, he just knew he couldn't go home and face the embarrassment of failing college, so he decided to head south to Louisiana where his aunt Dedria and her new husband Robert offered to take him in for a time.

A few years before, Aubrey met a girl at church camp from Minden, Louisiana. Her family also opened up to Aubrey and, between both homes Aubrey had found a new sense of security for himself. He had felt that this open door and the support he was receiving was going to allow him to face his failure. Even with this overwhelming sense of support, Aubrey still found himself empty, and confused about his future. One can have a void in their life from many different things. Unhealed hurts, unresolved issues, blatant sin and rebellion, trauma or generational issues, the list can go on. We must begin to ask the question, "Why am I empty"? "What has brought me to this place in my life?" Aubrey knew the answer to such questions but is unwilling to answer them.

In just a short time in Louisiana he came to the conclusion that it would be best to enter the Navy. And even this decision came as a result of a stumbled upon conclusion.

In his description of the process, Aubrey explains the following:

"It was the end of 2007 and I was living with my Aunt. It was my cousin Heston's senior year. He gets the wild idea that after high school concluded, he was joining the Navy. I was so sure that he wouldn't do it that I told him that if he did it, I would do it.

Shortly after the new year in 2008, I receive a phone call telling me that Heston signed the papers and had committed to the US Navy. I thought of the many ways to get out of it, but I had backed out of everything else in life. Maybe this was my chance to figure out what I wanted in life. So that next week, I went to the recruiter and decided to enlist. I scored really high on the ASVAB, so I had my choice of jobs and many to choose from.

At this time the movie "The Guardian" with Kevin Costner and Ashton Kutcher was very popular. Rescue Swimmer was the option, and I thought "that could be me saving people," I would be a hero! I was always looking for something that would set me apart and make people proud of me. Talking with the recruiters they made me feel like life would be set for me once boot camp was over: 1. I would be respected. 2. I would save lives. 3. I would never be stuck on a boat. I should not have been so naive, because that's the exact opposite of what I found out.

After boot camp, I was expecting life to get easier. Nope! It got worse! I also found out that my instructor at Rescue Swimmer School had saved only 6 people in 14 years, and most of the time, Rescue Swimmers are always stationed on ships. All that I was led to believe was a lie, and I thought my recruiter was my friend. So, first chance I got to come back to see him I found out he had retired. I was one of the last recruits he needed, so he told me what I wanted to hear."

Everyone in the family was supporting him and was also very proud of him.   Off course there would be the opportunity for the Marine to give Aubrey a hard time when they would talk on the phone. At this point Austin, was full time in the Marine Corps, ever increasing in leadership and making his way up the chain of command.   There was a small part of Aubrey crying out for support of the decision that he made.   He received that support, and there was a sense of pride beginning to develop in his heart, but it was still not enough to fill any level of empty space.   There was still an encounter that would have to come to his heart and to his life.

When Aubrey entered the Navy, he did not have any idea what area he wanted to serve in. After basic training, he set is eyes on becoming a Rescue Diver. The search for significance was so large in Aubrey that he felt that if he could become a rescue diver then he would be admired and looked up to. What Aubrey had not realized, is that he was already significant in the eyes of a loving Heavenly Father.

This realization is constantly chasing each and every one of us. God loves each and every one of us. The love is so significant that He gave His only Son to die on the cross for our sin. That, my friends, is the most significant act of love in all of mankind. When he looks at you, when he looks at Aubrey, He sees significance.

And now, during Aubrey's Navy Journey, he finds himself in training. A training that would be a moment for Aubrey to face his fear. As he is under the water, the tornados of the past continue to spin.

Nothing is going right. He begins to ask himself "how did I get here?" "What have I done with my life?" As water starts to fill his lungs he begins kicking and trying everything he can to break loose; when, everything fades to black. In the midst of the blackness, Aubrey finds himself outside of his father's car, looking at the accident that had changed his life forever. Amid the darkness, he sees flashing lights and noise of people. As he gazed into the darkness of his thoughts, he still is at that place of a lost little boy looking upon the death of his father. That night, fear stepped into his life and robbed him of his faith. In that moment, if he could have spoken it out under water, he would have yelled out, "God if you will help me get out of this, I will change."

When Aubrey comes to and gasps for air, he is lying beside the pool. Eyes open, and air filling his lungs. Aubrey survived something that could have ended in tragedy. This event added to the initial fear placed in his spirit the night of his father's tragic accident.

Aubrey sat up with a dazed look in his eyes. He stood to his feet and immediately his Senior Chief walks up to him and said, "Anderson, are you okay?"

Aubrey replied, "Yes, I think I am."

The last thing that Aubrey wanted to show was any sign weakness, knowing it would cost him if he did.

Senior Chief responded again, "Are you ready to go again?"

Aubrey responded, "I don't know if I can".

"If you don't go again, you will not finish your training. You can go tomorrow with the next group," the Senior Chief said.

"Okay Senior Chief", Aubrey replied with a thankfulness that he did not have to go again that day.   As soon as Aubrey left the pool, he called Austin.

"What's up bro." Austin answered.

"I almost died today" Aubrey said.

"You did not," Austin exclaimed.

"Yes, I did!" and began to explain to Austin the events that unfolded moments before the phone call. "I just don't know if I have what it takes to do it again," Aubrey said.

"Man listen, you have always had what it takes, and I believe in you. Remember you are an Anderson, we don't quit." Austin replied. Austin went on to say, "You remember the night of Dad's accident, you got yourself out of the car and you walked down the road with broken ankles? You made it through that, and you can make it through this. Don't you quit!"

The next day Aubrey got up and prepared for the training, with high levels of anxiety and fear. He stepped into the pool doing everything he could possibly do, to not think about the failure of the day before. He followed every instruction given to him and finds himself in the very same seat, in the same position as the day before. The lever is pulled, and the helo-dunker splashed into the water, and spins upside down. Aubrey, while maintaining a hold on his seat, unbuckles the harness and swims to the exit.

As Aubrey made his way to the surface, was relieved that the harness did not stick, he was jubilant, nobody else was as excited as he was. For a moment, Aubrey realized that he could master anything if he would just put his mind to it. Training continued for Aubrey, swimming thousands of meters each week. Three days a week, he would have to do 5- mile beach runs. He was constantly training and moving forward, until Aubrey started to experience pain in his back. After going to the Naval doctor, he was diagnosed with kidney stones. That diagnosis would put a stop to Aubrey's training. After weeks of waiting to return to training, Aubrey was finally cleared to go back. The news that was awaiting Aubrey's return would be one more setback in this young man's life.

"Anderson, you have been out of training too long. You are going to be dropped from the Rescue Swimmer Program." Senior Chief said.

With a million thoughts flooding Aubrey's mind, the only thing that he could muster, "Okay Senior!"

Leaving that conversation, Aubrey went back to the barracks. With the feeling of being rejected, and even abandoned, and ultimately confused, the tornado continued to spin.

A group of guys were going out that evening to a bar, and even though Aubrey was shy of twenty-one years old, he went. There was a friend that Aubrey had in his unit that looked a lot like him. He was twenty-one and they decided to let Aubrey used his I.D. As far as Aubrey was concerned, he had nothing to lose.

When the group returned to the barracks, they dragged Aubrey in. He was past done and definitely had one too many, or in this case, five too many. They loudly brought Aubrey in, and because of the commotion caused, Aubrey was picked out of the group to be in trouble. He is the only one that is under age. They made Aubrey stand at attention (as much as possible) on the deck awaiting the arrival of his Senior Chief. Aubrey had enough sense to him that he was highly concerned that he could go to jail for what he had just done, or even more, that he could be kicked out of the Navy. Senior Chief arrives and steps in front of Seaman Anderson.

"Anderson what did you do?"

Aubrey replied, "Had a little too much to drink Senior!"   "How old are you?" Senior Chief shouted.

"I am 20 Senior!" Aubrey said back.

"How can you be so stupid, you are what is wrong with the Navy today! What were you thinking?" Senior Chief asked.

"I was not thinking, Senior!" replied Aubrey.

"You are definitely not going to be a rescue swimmer now! How stupid can you be! I have seen people make stupid decisions, but this one takes the top!" The Senior yelled.

In the midst of the Senior yelling these statements, there is no response of visible care from Aubrey.

"Do you think your family would be proud of you right now?"

Aubrey did not have a response anymore.   The Senior Chief kept digging at him and Aubrey was ready to take it. The Senior continued to tell Aubrey how stupid he was.

"The best part of you ran down your mothers leg a stain on the mattress. That is what you are, a stain on your mother's mattress."

Rage and anger rose up in Aubrey, and he took a swing, aiming at the Senior Chief's face, but being inebriated, the punch missed, and that swing set a course for the seaman that he did not want to take. Aubrey is now out of Rescue Swimmer school and headed to a classification of undesignated and placed at the mercy of the navy.   No purpose, plan undone, and once again very alone.   The tornado still spins.

One month later, Aubrey was stationed on the U.S.S. Enterprise. Aubrey is focused on finishing strong, staying out of trouble and making the best of a bad situation.   He was designated to the V-4 division, which is Aviation Boatswain's Mate, fuels. They operate, maintain, and perform organizational maintenance on aviation fueling and lubrication systems. After serving two tours on the Enterprise, Aubrey was able to see Greece, Spain, Turkey, Portugal, Bahrain, and many miles of blue ocean.   Aubrey worked his way to the flight deck and served his time.   Aubrey's second deployment was the final deployment for the USS Enterprise. When Aubrey finished the Navy well and was one of the highest qualified E-3 in the V-4 division.

On April 12, 2012, Aubrey finished his deployment and service in the Navy. He arrived at home, thankful that he finally made it.   Four years coming out of this season was a breath of fresh air to Aubrey. Even with a fresh season and excitement to be free of what felt like a prison sentence, Aubrey was longing for direction.

Aubrey is taking time to work out and enjoy his pay from the military and going to clubs, and just enjoying life, hiding from the fact that he had to find his next step.

Aubrey decides to go and help Austin move.   Once again Austin begins to question Aubrey with the same questions.   What are you doing? Aubrey's response was the same, "I have no idea".

Stephen, Luke, Austin, Elizabeth and Aubrey went to go eat after moving Austin. Austin asked Aubrey to move to Tyler, encouraging him to find work there and go to school.   Austin was going to help Aubrey find his destination and place.   Austin was set on a mission not only to help his sister Allie, but if he could get Aubrey to get dedicated to something, anything, then he felt like he was accomplishing something bigger than himself.

Little did Aubrey know that these moments with his brother would soon change. His future would consist of only wishing for the constant nudging of brotherly advice. But for now, in this moment, the tornado continued to spin.

It was April of 1994, and many from Faith Center were attending a large meeting in Oklahoma City. The downtown Myriad Convention Center was packed with thousands of people in anticipation of the evening meeting. The Worship at this event was truly moving, and without a doubt, the very presence of the Lord was present. It was like a thick blanket was resting upon every life. You couldn't see it, but you could sense it and feel that it was tangible.

Many people walk through their entire journey with Christ never knowing His divine and ever present, presence. That is what His Holy Spirit, the third part of the Trinity, will do for everyone who opens up their life to a deeper walk with Christ. He gives each one of us more of His presence. It is so incredible when you think about it. God loves each and every one of us so much that He gives us His Holy Spirit to allow us to know that He is ever present. In addition to that, the Bible tells us that He is our ever-present help in time of need. How does He do that? By His Holy Spirit. Honestly, why would we ever say, "I don't need the Holy Spirit?" No way! We need all of His divine presence. We need the Holy Spirit at work in every area our lives. We should never settle for enough but seek more. All of you God, all of your presence at work in every area of my life. When that type of desire unfolds in our hearts, God responds, and on this day, God was responding.

Cody and Monte were walking on the floor and were waved to by another Pastor that was seated on the platform. He told Monte that there were seats in front that two people could sit in. Mary insisted that Monte and Cody take those seats and she would go sit with the rest of the Faith Center family that was there. Monte and Cody take their seats and enjoy the worship and the presence of God moving in the midst of this service.

In the midst of this meeting, the guest speaker looked into the crowd. Making eye contact with Monte, he motioned for him to come up. Here in the midst of thousands of people, Monte became the focal point of the arena, and what took place next was the unveiling of a hunger and a passion for the presence of God that would consume Monte for all of his life. The speaker silences all of the music and began to tell Monte that he was in a wide-open place, a place that few would go.

Faith Center is a church that is in the middle of no-where Oklahoma. Wide open spaces all around, and the town where this vibrant church sits is in a community of less than 200 people.

The speaker looked at Monte and said this, "You are expecting a baby soon is that correct?" Monte responded, "Yes sir it is."

"It will be a girl with blonde hair and blue eyes and she will bring you great joy." the speaker said.

Some may think that strange, and no it was nothing new age, or fortune telling, but it was the sincere word of knowledge by the Holy Spirit, delivered by grace through a man. Even more than that, it was God showing the details of how much He cares.

You see Mary was pregnant, and that which would come forth is a baby girl who was blonde haired and blue eyed, and with the middle name "Joy". Allie Joy Anderson came not only as the joy of her father, but the fulfillment of a word by the Holy Spirit of God. It was not only confirmation that she would bring joy, but God was saying to Monte, "I see you, I care for you and I just want you to know that I am into the details of your life."

This beautiful blonde hair, blue eyed girl captured the heart of the entire family. Always smiling, always laughing and yet quiet. She sat watching everyone and everything around her. Only five years old when Monte passed away, the joy was hard to find, and the tensions of this journey became so hard and difficult to walk. Allie loved her dad with all of heart and being. If Monte was home, he was either hugging her or loving on her, holding her on his lap.   The hug was gone, the lap was not present to sit on, the words of his voice, and sound of his songs that he would sing to her are all absent.

Mary had built the new house for the kids shortly after Monte passed. Allie really thought that this new home was her own castle.

When it came to Disney movies, this family owned all the classics. As you well know, at the beginning of each Disney movie is the view of the castle. Because that castle was blue, and the new house was painted blue, and sitting on a beautiful hill, Allie thought that this was her castle, and that she was the princess of it.   She probably was if the truth were to be known. What Allie wanted, just like every last born of the family, she probably got. Her brothers would attest to that fact. Everything was about Allie. When it was time to eat, it wasn't what the boys wanted, but it was about what Allie would eat. A family with the absence of one is doing everything they can to establish something new and build with the fragments of what is left to create an atmosphere of faith, hope and love.   They would all work so hard physically and emotionally toward that very thing, but no matter how hard they would try to accomplish that, it just wasn't happening.

There was a red rocking recliner that Mary had purchased and placed in the living room. It was a large recliner, and Mary, Austin, Aubrey, and little Allie would try to sit in it and rock.   That recliner would be the place where Mary would start many mornings in.   A place of reflection, prayer, and weeping.   A place of refuge, but also a place of pain and desperation.   One evening, Mary was rocking Allie, just holding her. Austin had chosen to move out with Papa and Annie, a decision that was very difficult for everyone. As they rock into the night, Mary told Allie, "There will be a day when it is just going to be you and I."

Mary began to cry and Allie with her precious blue eyes, looked up to her mother and hugged her and nestled into her, falling asleep.

Mary had stretched out of her comfort zone to begin dating. It was not easy and there is no way that anyone could replace Monte. His character, just who he was, could never be replaced. The children struggled with it very much.   The tension between the boys and Mary began to grow as different individuals made attempts to come into their lives. Tensions were growing so much that Aubrey decided for his senior year that it would be best for him to move into Papa and Annie's house as well.   Austin had left for the Marine Corps, and the overwhelming sense of change that was coming at this family created such adversity and challenge that it was easier for everyone to just be by themselves.

This blonde hair, blue eyed girl watched so much evolve in her life in a matter of three years, and everyone close to her was leaving. The outer shell of beauty was not the same picture on the inside. Allie was lonely, abandoned and struggling, but she loved her mom and was there for her. The number of nights that Mary would cry herself to sleep outnumbered the nights of peace. Allie Joy had a difficult time grasping the joy when what surrounded her was loneliness, weeping and frustration. Mary would do everything possible to make her laugh and do things with her and have friends over for her.

For Mary, people are what she loved, and she loved having as many people around as she could. When people were present, she and Allie were not alone. They did not have to think about what was gone, or who was missing. It works great, but people still leave and have to go home. When everyone is gone, it is still silent, and it is still an empty house.

You can build something in the hopes that it will fill what you desire. You can build a frame and complete the walls and place furnishings in it, but it still lacks being a home. This castle of Allies became a place of despair and loneliness.   Mary decided that she and Allie needed a new start at a new place and made the decision to move to Enid. Mary told Allie that this move was better for her new job, which she loved. Mary had become a massage therapist, working in Enid. However, she still wanted to leave Ringwood, wanted to leave the church and everything that held a memory for the past.

A new start, a new beginning and everything would be better. Allie was heart-broken. The friends that she had built for 5 years of school, she was walking away from. Her family, the church that she loved to attend, they were leaving behind anything familiar for Mary, but Allie didn't fully grasp why.

There were friends across the street that attended the new school where Allie was attending but it was still hard. She missed home, she missed what was her little castle in the trees, she missed her brothers. Austin would write to her and tell her that he loved her, and that he could not wait to see her again. Austin would tell her over and over again, "Allie, I did not leave because of you, I love you, everything will be alright." Austin was getting ready to finish basic training in the Marine Corps. In the midst of being gone, he always reminded Allie that he loved her.

In the midst of loss, words that come from those who are close to us have a greater volume, and they carry a tremendous amount of weight to them. That is why many walking through our loss, will be more emotional towards those who are close to us because we are just simply more sensitive. That is natural, and it is okay. We must realize that words matter. Austin's consistent words of support, strength and love towards Allie were words that had great volume to her heart. Allie viewed Austin as the image of her dad. Austin would be the one that would pick her up and hold her, hug her and be the voice of strength.   The image that Allie held onto towards Austin, was an image that was probably larger than life, he could do no wrong and he could take on anything in this world and conquer it.

Amid loss, it so vital for each of us to realize that God uses people to speak life into us, we can't shut everyone off.   What they say can be a source of help to us in the journey.   Just the opposite is true, if we listen to the wrong people their words can do damage to our hearts and emotions. In earlier chapters we have highlighted the fact that the Bible tells us in the book of James, our words matter. It can be words that lead to life or they can be words that lead to death. In our journey, we need people in our life that will speak life to us and give us an image to hold onto in the journey. Austin was that person in Allie's life.

Austin is in his final steps to complete basic training in San Diego, California. The entire family goes out to California for his graduation, excited to see Austin. It has been too long, and the family is waiting with great expectation to see their strong Marine. They arrive at the Marine Corps Recruit Depot in San Diego and stand in the California sun and watch the new recruits march in. Cody puts Allie on his shoulders, so she can see Austin.   The crowd was huge, and one would really have to focus in to see their family member make the march in.   All of their eyes lock in on Austin, and tears begin to fill their eyes as they finally picked him out of the sea of Marines marching that day.

Allie started to cry and said, "What happened to Austin".

When they say that Marines are mean, lean, fighting machines, that is an understatement. Austin had lost an incredible amount of weight. He looked as if he had been in a concentration camp. The bones in his forehead were sticking out, face so thin, and not one ounce of body fat anywhere in him. Austin had gotten extremely sick towards the end of his basic training. He did not stop, continuing to press through to complete the difficult task of becoming a Marine and finishing his training. He did not even look the same and everyone, most of all Allie, was in shock. She was concerned that they had changed him. So many things were already different for her, and she was afraid that Austin would not be the same. Once reunited, it did not take long for her to see that the strength she gathered from Austin was still there and the support was still present in this strong Marine. For Allie, Austin was still the stable and consistent support that she needed.

Allie loved the trip to California because she was able to travel with all her family. She loved being under the same roof with her cousins and Annie and Papa. She loved being at the beach and being with the ones that she loved and cared for. She missed it, and a sense of being with family and being with Austin brought happiness to her heart.

Once back home from California, Mary had been working on some additional plans to further her career and schooling as a Massage Therapist. These plans would take yet another move to Norman, Oklahoma. Good plans for Mary and added support from her family would be something Mary needed and would be good for her and Allie. Even though it was a good plan, it was a hard move for Allie, because it was further away from what was familiar and from the things and people she loved. Allie would thrive around new friends and support from Mary's family that was close by. Even though she missed home and the family she had grown up with she was fitting in and living life.

You know we can all fit in and wake up every day and just live life. Millions of people do that every day and it works for a while. When we don't receive healing from the loss, healing from the pain, or healing from the emptiness, there will be a day that we start our day and realize we are still alone, we are still in pain, and we don't know what to do. Or even worse we just make ourselves numb to life. Mary, on countless nights, would still cry herself to sleep. Allie would still just rest in that red rocking recliner with her mom, still feeling alone, still longing for everything to be better than what it was.

Austin is still in the Marine Corps and not around at all. Aubrey has now joined the Navy and he is not around. Alone with her mother who she so deeply loved, but something is still missing, something is still absent from her life and she has no idea what it is. As Allie grew with age, and now in High School, the way that she dealt with the gaping hole in her heart was to be in the crowd. In the crowd deep. To keep Allie safe, Mary would tell her to bring friends to the house, don't go out. But Allie wanted to do more than just have friends over, she wanted to drink alcohol. She discovered something that would make her numb to what was missing. Numb to the men that would date her mom, that were not her dad, they were not Austin, and numb to the fact that she longed to be home. Home for Allie was not the place of home, but the idea of home. Familiar things that made her feel that she was not missing anything.

Here is the difficulty with desiring to get something that is familiar to make us feel better. We are dealing with a hole in our heart that only God can heal. We are dealing with an emptiness that even familiar things will not be able to fill. People make those statements all the time. Let go and let God, but what does that really mean? It is very difficult to walk that out in our mind and emotions. The truth is, God can, and He will comfort us when we are in the midst of loss. You honestly can't explain it, but when you stop trying to make yourself numb to what you are missing, you then realize that it will never be the same again. It just won't. That is the truth, we cannot go back in time, we just get tomorrow. By the comfort of His presence, and the work of the Holy Spirit in our lives we realize that we are not alone and that He is for us. He strengthens us. The Word of God changes how we view our circumstance. Listen, God never promises in His Word that we will not face challenges in this life. This world is broken, and we are in it. Brokenness will come our way. The question is, do we keep trying to stay numb to it, or do we realize that only God can give us what we have need of? Not a person, not a substitute, not one thing in this earth can do it, only He can.

Allie is looking, she is longing for what is missing and drinking and being a part of the party was filling the void. This lifestyle was tearing her apart and damaging the relationship with her mother. Mary did not like it, but in some respects, she just did not have any fight in her. Both of her sons were away, and the last thing that she wanted was to fight or do anything that would cause Allie not to be happy.   In the midst of Mary's weariness and being tired, both become heartbroken even deeper.   Allie and Mary were living, but not really living happy. Broken hearts were not getting mended and pain was rising between all of them.

Mary so desired to see healing. She never took her eyes off of the Word of God, she would pray every day and there would not be a day in which she would not journal what she was believing for and what she was feeling. No matter how much Mary would do, relations with her children just would not get to the place of healing. They loved each other very much and there was no doubt about that, but they would fight and argue more and more. Four people now growing into adults and Allie approaching 17 years of age becoming a young adult. All of them, still looking for healing to what was broken. All of them dealing with loss. All of them attempting to fix what was broken. It is a very interesting thing that often times unfold for each of us. The things we long to fix in our lives are also the things we fight against. Every one of them wanted a better relationship with one another.

Please catch this reality. You can't truly give to someone else in a relationship when you are empty and hurting. This is why it is so critical that we understand that from a place of being healed and restored we are not guarded, we give instead of taking all the time. Hurting people, hurt people! When you have a household of hurting people, everyone stays and gets hurt. When you are healed you stop trying to protect yourself against everything and everyone. You are ready to give, you are ready to put others above yourself.

Allie wanted to stay numb and being around friends and friends that would support her drinking and other things, kept her numb, and Mary was not about to do anything that would keep her from being happy. Allie was getting good at building walls around herself. Allie wanted to run but did not know where she could run to. It wasn't about running from Mary, Allie just wanted to run. She wanted Austin, but that is not what she really wanted, she wanted strength, security and those things that made her feel safe. Even amid struggling, Mary was dedicated to go to church and make sure that Allie went on Sunday's to service. It was that longing for God to come and help, but still not enough for Allie. She was struggling to open up in such a way that healing could come. Instead of opening up, it was easier to build walls.

You know we can be in the atmosphere for change and not change. We can be sitting next to the answer and not even see it. Why? Pain blinds us to the help we so desperately need. That is why pain, emptiness, loneliness, loss, desperation, you name it, can cloud our vision. Allie's vision was clouded, and the answer to her pain could not be seen. She needed to be in a place to see clearer and to know that God loved her and that He alone needed to be that strength for her, not her dad, not even Austin, not her mother. But God! Only God!

Austin was back in the area. He was attending Oral Roberts University, and at the end of his pursuit of his degree in Business. He was still serving in the Reserves, but that too was coming to an end. He would come to Norman and lay in bed with Allie and they would watch their favorite movies. Austin would do everything he could to help Allie and talk about her future. He wanted so desperately to take Allie with him to school. For Mary, that would be too much to be alone.

Mary started having some issues with her heart, some irregular heartbeats and at certain times, Mary's breath would be taken back. She did not know what was going on, but something was wrong. In the midst of Mary needing extra help with Allie because she didn't feel well, Austin would come and get Allie just to spend time with her.

He would get permission from Mary to go back to spend the weekend at Ringwood. Allie loved the ranch, they would ride horseback across the ranch and ride along the creek and gaze upon the river. Having been six years since attending, Allie returned to services at Faith Center. So much had changed and she loved being there for the service. Something was shifting in Allie, there was a light that was beginning to come through the darkness and emptiness of her heart.

Austin loved the ranch as well, he loved talking about life plans with Allie on the ranch. Austin had an incredible plan for everyone, and his plans were going to work for him and for her, and for Aubrey and for Mary. He had it all figured out! Those life talks with Allie forever impacted her and it began something. There was a strength that was returning and a sense of purpose that was unfolding.

Back in Norman a few weeks after this great weekend getaway to the ranch, Mary was doing better, and their house was filled with friends. In the midst of all the noise and laughter, Allie walked into her room and finds Mary reading her diary.

"Mom, what are you doing"? Allie asks.

Mary responds, "Allie, I know that you are engaging in certain things and I just wanted to make sure you are being safe".

"That is private, and you have no right to look at it!" Allie screams.

The entire house that was once full of noise and laughter went into a silent mode, and the crowd began to leave as Mary and Allie continued to argue about what had just transpired.   Allie grabs a few things out of her room and storms out the front door. Mary thought that Allie had gone outside to cool down, but Allie was bent on running away.   Allie calls Austin in the middle of the night.

"Austin, I can't take being in this house anymore, please come get me," Allie cries.

Hearing his sister crying and knowing the desperation of her heart, he did not hesitate to come. Allie had one of her friends take her to meet Austin. As Austin was on the way to get Allie, he called Mary. Following a long conversation, Mary agreed to let Austin take Allie for a few more days until things cooled down between them.

Even if a home is full of people, full of laughter and activity, the chaos can keep us moving forward, but without peace the chaos will eventually cause an implosion. Emotions implode, and words can cause damaging effects. Right now, this home is imploding, and everyone involved is hurting and empty.   Healing and restoration are behind a wall.

Austin had spent a lot of time in thought these few days about his plan to take Allie to Texas with him, figuring she could finish her Senior year with him. He would do everything he could to make it better for her. Not that he knew what would be better, but if he could help his sister and his mother both find a place of peace, he would do it. Allie felt safe with Austin. The safety she felt with him was because of his strength, and throughout all her life, Austin was the one who would protect her, and help her when she needed it. The truth is this, Allie was looking for something in Austin, and in others that could never be fulfilled by him. Man can never give unto us what God has created for Him and Him only to provide: Peace and Comfort.

There were many missions that Austin was on and one of the most important missions was Allie. To give her what he felt she needed, to support her and help her find purpose. In the midst of his mission he also knew that there needed to be something healthier developed in the relationship between Mary and Allie. After a few days, cooler hearts, and minds prevailing, he took Allie back home to Norman. Both Allie and Mary were ready to bury the hatchet and move past a moment of anger and confusion. Mary continued to share with Allie that all she wanted was to make sure Allie was safe and doing things that were safe for her and others around. The drama had passed, and things were good, but Allie kept looking for a way to fill the emptiness, to be in a place of peace in her heart and life. Austin had to return to ORU and prepare for his finals and Senior projects that were due. Good news was coming to Allie and Mary, Aubrey was coming home, and his time with the Navy was coming to an end.

Even though Mary and Allie had overcome a temporary situation, and Allie kept doing things that were not the best for her, Mary allowed her to drink just to be able to monitor when it was too much. Mary would tell her, "I don't agree with what you are doing, but I am here for you and I would rather you drink here, rather than somewhere, I do not know where you are".

Mary chose to help in the way she felt was going to be the most beneficial to Allie. But Allie was searching and was not able to find the answer she was looking for.

Now that Aubrey was back home, the drinking just became something normal for the house. Both Aubrey and Allie would drink. Mary knowing that they each had to cope with their hurt and emptiness somehow, just wanted them home where she felt they were safe. If that meant letting them get by with certain things, then fine. Finding peace would be the aim of Mary's heart, going to great lengths to keep the kids close to her. They are with her and that is what matters. She did not approve of things they were doing, and she was not afraid to voice her concern for some of Aubrey's and Allie's decisions, but she hated to argue with them. Mary was simply tired.

It is a fine line as a parent that we draw sometimes. "I desire to be your friend, but my friendship cannot take place of the authority that has been entrusted to me." The authority that is there to protect you from making decisions that will be hurtful to you.

Let's be perfectly honest, there is not one person on the face of the planet that likes being told we are wrong, or that the decision we are making is not going to be healthy for us. True love holds us not just when we are hurting or in pain, but love confronts things in our life that will be best for us in the long run. There is a statement that is made a lot of times, "It is time for tough love." This looks different for everybody and there are some that take that statement and go too far with it. Confrontation, when done in love and grace, can help those in whom we care for, make decisions that will keep them from devastating results. At this point there is no one in this home wanting to confront or is accepting any level of confrontation. When things stay hidden in the dark, nothing changes.

Allie stands by the street outside her home making phone calls to anyone who could possibly come and get her. She was done, she was finished, and was ready to get away from home. She gets ahold of Austin and begs him to come and get her. Austin makes the two-hour drive from Tulsa to Norman to pick up his little sister. Austin would do anything at a moment's notice for Allie.

Austin called his uncle Cody. "Allie has called me, and she says that she wants to come live with me, she wants out of Norman."

Cody responds, "Get her picked up and take her back to Tulsa. Call your mother and tell her what is going on and just to let you take her for the weekend."

Austin called Mary and she agreed to let Austin take her for the weekend.   Austin decided to bring Allie back to the ranch. For the both of them, it was a place of refuge, a place where things were at peace with their heart, a place where they could hold onto a sense of peace in the midst of the chaos of their thoughts and emotions.

Austin convinced Allie that she not only needed her mother, but that Mary needed her as well. Aubrey was at home in Norman now and together they could work together to help each other receive love, and to be strong.   Allie went back to Norman, but she still was not settled in her heart that Norman was where she needed to be. She knew that at any time, Austin would be there for her. If she needed anything then the tall, blonde headed, blue eyed Marine would come to her rescue. Austin was her hero. Austin would yet prove that he was that hero.

May 2012. Austin had solidified his decision to move forward with his plans to graduate from Oral Roberts University. Having proudly served two tours in Iraq, it was now time to become employed as a civilian. He would file the paper work to complete his service as a Marine. The shift from protecting the world to changing it, had begun. That is Austin Anderson in a nut shell, a world changer, and everyone around him would gladly affirm.

During his time there, Austin had built strong relationships at ORU. He thrived on the campus, and there was a reciprocal appreciation and respect between he and his professors. One professor in the Business College must have captured a special place in Austin's heart. And when I say "heart", I mean cardio-vascular system. Austin found a commercial grade treadmill that he single-handedly hauled up the stairs to the professor's office. Why? Because Austin thought this particular professor needed to get more exercise. Now he would have no excuse. That is a fairly good description of Austin Anderson.

Austin was a part of the cheerleading squad at ORU. Let me repeat that just so you don't think it was a misprint. Yes, as big and soldier like as he was, Austin was a part of the cheerleading team. He took pride in this position. Not because of his passion for cheering, but rather because it offered him a place to use his strengths to clear the pathway to his purpose. Austin would do anything for a scholarship, so when they offered him one for cheering, he gladly took it. At first, they loved having him because of his strength and dedication. It wasn't long before that love turned into a physically exhausted "like." He was always getting them to work out as if they were Marines, and that was not always popular with everyone on the squad. That stopped Austin zero percent.

This season produced great friends like Stephen Luth (who also served with Austin on the ORU Cheer squad), Garrett Coble (who became a close confidant to Austin) and Luke Sheets. Another dear friendship to Austin was a young lady named Hanna Luce, as well as a vast list of others that would render this book three additional chapters had we included them. From professors, to Veterans Affairs, to Administration, to cheer squad, to workers behind the scenes at Oral Roberts University, the list is one of expansion not conclusion.

Out of all the relationships he had, there was one that was of the utmost importance in his eyes. This was his relationship with Elizabeth. This relationship had grown and was becoming much more than just dating, it was ranch worthy. You see, anytime someone gets invited to the ranch to meet the family, this means it is getting very serious. Due to the fact that the ranch was always a place of home for Austin, anyone invited there under this type of category of relationship was considered to be potential family. From its Oklahoma sprawl setting, to spending time with Papa, his love for the ranch ran deep. Getting approval from Annie and Papa, Uncle Cody and Aunt Amy was part of the interview process for any girlfriend. Elizabeth passed the test!

Everyone loved Elizabeth.   There were very few people that could stop Austin and get him to be quiet. Elizabeth had a way to get his attention. There was no doubt that they would be awesome together.   Any time that Austin could pull it off with the time that he had, he would make it horse time. They would take rides along the creek and stop to talk about life, future, and the plans Austin had. Austin had so many plans and the future's potential was so bright. Elizabeth knew how to handle this big lug of a guy, and you could tell by looking in their eyes that, they had a deep, growing love for each other.

Austin's friend Hannah Luce is the daughter of Ron Luce. Ron is the founder of Teen Mania Ministries. Hannah had shared with her father the influence of this world changer named Austin Anderson. Mr. Luce wanted to meet Austin, and when they did Mr. Luce saw something that he liked. Ron then offered Austin a position on his team as the Vice President of operations for Teen Mania Ministries.

Austin was beyond excited about the opportunity. Austin had gone to countless number of Acquire the Fire (hosted by Teen Mania Ministries) events as youth. He loved and had a passion for this style and genre of ministry, and was so excited that immediately following graduation, he would be on a team that was impacting the world.

Graduation at Oral Roberts University is moving. It is not only celebratory, but it is full of the presence of God. The entire Anderson family has shown up in full force to support this proud Marine as he receives his diploma at the University of his dreams. What a day it was! Full of tears of joy with Mary, Allie and Aubrey, who, only days prior had just returned from completing his time of service in the Navy. Everyone was happy to be celebrating this milestone event for Austin. The only word that can capsulize the shared, heartfelt emotion is proud.

Austin had already moved some of his things from Oklahoma to Texas, where he would start his new beginning in the major league of changing the world. It was all coming to pass in his life, and he was full of excitement to be embarking upon the career and call that he had dreamed. Graduating from ORU was something that he wanted to complete, not only for himself, but as a memorial of honor for his father Monte. And so, he did.

He gathered up the last of his things and was going to fly from Tulsa, OK to Council Bluff, Iowa for a Teen Mania Youth Rally. This was his first review of how procedures were being done, and he was ready to evaluate and develop new strategies that would bring about growth to the ministry. Austin was ready to change the world one rally, one event, one stadium at a time.

He organized the trip and the plane was reserved and ready to go. His friends were going to go with him on the trip. His hope was for some of his friends to consider being a part of the team that he was building. This would be a good way to expose them to the potential roles that may reveal themselves to be filled. Luke Sheets was asked to fly, and Garret Coble and Stephen Luth were going to see what possibilities might unfold for them.

Hannah Luce decided to go on the trip and then return to Tulsa with this crew of friends. Austin was going to help Hannah move the rest of her things back to Texas from Tulsa. Everything was set, and they were ready to go.   Austin made a call to his Uncle Cody.

"Uncle Cody," he said. Cody could tell the excitement in his voice. "We are getting ready to go in a little while."

"I am excited for you, is Elizabeth going with you?" asked Cody.

Austin replies, "No she is not. She is, however, going to drive home and on her way home she is going to stop in Council Bluffs and see us before we return back to Tulsa."

"That is good, I am sure that you are excited about this event." Cody said.

" Yes, I can't wait to get there, and I can't wait to see what happens in the upcoming weeks for Teen Mania. I want to help Ron," said Austin.

"We will pray for you and have a safe flight," Cody said.

"Hey, Uncle Cody can I ask you a question?" asked Austin.

"Sure," Cody replied.

"I think I have a ring picked out for Elizabeth, do you think that December would be a good time for a wedding?" Austin asked.

Cody laughed and said, "I bet it will a be perfect time."

Austin replied, "I do too! I will call you when we land in Council Bluffs."

"Okay, I love you man and I am proud of you," said Cody.

Shortly after this call, they climbed onto the plane and took off from Jones Airport in Jenks, Oklahoma.   Full of life and excitement, these young leaders, in fact we will call it like it is; world changers were beginning to build a future. Creating strategies of growth and expansion and how they could do it better. The Elisha's were on their way to walk in the double portion of anointing handed to them. They were walking as if they had received the prophetic mantel from Elijah. Incredible passion to change the world one life at a time. As they flew, it became a little cool in the plane and they told them to turn the heater on. Continuing their conversations, they were unaware that this would be the moment everything changed.

We are never ready for moments of change. We can't say all the time but the majority of the time, circumstances are thrust upon us. There is no way to ever prepare for them. They show up unannounced. They appear out of nowhere. If we ever think for one moment that we can be prepared for every circumstance, then we are living in a naive state of mind. In fact, we are lost without a God center.   In other words, we have no sense of life or death and the consequences of both.

You see, when God is at the center of our life, we are better equipped and ready for what is thrust upon us. When God is at the center of our will and our life, then in our heart of hearts, deep within us, we possess a greater ability to see things different. This life is not about us, but it is about Him.   Life becomes about pleasing the Lord no matter what unfolds.   When God is at the center, we have the ability and confidence to close our eyes and be okay if circumstances are thrust upon us that lead to the end of this life. Is God at the center of your life or is it just you? If God is at the center, then Jesus has been made the Lord over all areas of your life, and you are born again. If you are at the center of your life, then you are all you have. If you close your eyes today in a circumstance that is thrust upon you that leads you to the end of this life, my friend you will not see Jesus on the other side of that circumstance.   We cannot waste any time, we just don't know what will be thrust upon us this very day.

The plane fills with smoke from the heater. The particular unit on this plane uses the planes fuel to flow through it to generate the heat.   The heater is malfunctioning and putting the fumes from the fuel into the cockpit and cabin of the plane. Luke begins to circle to find a safe place to land the plane. He sees an open field and attempts to make an emergency landing. They cover their mouths and nose to do everything they can to not breathe in the fumes as smoke is overtaking their ability to breathe. The door of the plane is opened in an attempt to get the fumes out, but it is not enough. The plane slams into the ground and slides into a row of trees on the edge of the field. As the plane's wing clips one of the trees and flips, the impact caused the plane to ignite and it was engulfed in flames. With the fuel flowing, the plane is totally consumed by the fire. Luke, Garret, and Stephen are lost upon the impact, if not before.

Hannah is burned over 30% of her body, still alive looking for help and hope. Austin is alive but barely breathing. He makes his way around the plane, brushing up against a five-wire fence with evidence of his skin on the fence itself, and his shoes melting off as he takes steps around the plane to see his friend Stephen laying in the plane. Austin makes his way into the flames to pull him out, but it was too much as he himself has been burned over 90% of his body. His clothes completely burned off of him and the fact that he was still standing is a miracle in itself. He then goes and helps Hannah and assists her.

Together they shockingly walk to a road that is over 100 yards from the site of the crash. Nearby, there was a woman driving the back roads of Kansas. She just purchased a hand gun and was going out to practice shooting. As a single mom, purchasing the pistol was a step of protection for her and her children. As she and a friend were going to find a place to shoot, they saw the smoke plume and quickly headed that way. When they arrived, Austin and Hannah were walking on the side of the road. When Austin and Hannah saw the car coming, they stopped walking. As the car approaches, there is nothing that can prepare them for what they are about to see. The sight was unbearable. The hair burnt off his head, Austin stood barefooted, and naked. The only thing that was not burned was the top of his feet. How he could even speak is a miracle at this point. One of them quickly calls 911 and the Neosho Fire and Rescue is dispatched to the scene.

These two wonderful and brave women begin to do all they can to assist Austin and Hannah. They had two bottles of water, and, when they tried to give Austin one, he said, "Take care of Hannah first." They tried to wrap a blanket around him but when it touched his body he yelled out in pain. They then decide to just hold it around him to cover his naked body. Minutes, which seemed like an eternity of time, went by and finally, emergency crews arrived.

The plane was still on fire in the field. Austin is loaded in one ambulance and Hannah is loaded in the another, as the life-saving work of this emergency crew did what they do best. Immediately they called for airlift. When asked whom to call, Austin was able to get out his Papa's number. As the emergency workers tried to work on Austin, they could not touch him without him yelling from the pain.   But in a moment of time he sat there, quiet and peaceful and they could not understand how he had so much peace. There was a presence there that day, in that hour, in that moment. It was the presence of the one who held the center of Austin's world. The presence of the Lord. It was Jesus!   After they laid him down and intubated him, he was not able to say another word.

Hannah Luce was taken to a Kansas City Hospital in critical condition. Austin was flown to Wichita and was beyond critical.   The phone rings and Cody picks it up. It was Annie.   "Austin's plane crashed, that is all we know."

"What?" Cody replied.

"We do not know any details, he is being transported to Wichita," said Annie.

With stern voice Cody asked, "Is he alive?"

Annie responded, "We don't know, but we do know he is critical."

The phone calls began to flood to one another. To Mary, Aubrey, and Allie, to other family, and family of the church. My God! We are here facing death once again and we can't believe it. We do not want this to be true, but this family is still praying and standing in hope.

Cody, Papa, and Annie, along with Mary, Allie, and Aubrey made the drive to Wichita as fast as they could. They pulled into the parking lot of the hospital at the same time. As each gets out of their vehicles, without a word being said, everyone embraces each other. They must stand in faith for a miracle.

As the family stepped into the room, their hearts fall apart. Their faith falls for a moment.   Austin is bandaged from top of his head to his ankles. The son of this family, this blue eyed, strong, and vibrant Marine is lying on this bed with no response, other than the machine that is breathing for him.   For hours, the family stands around his bed with tears of desperation and prayers of faith, fervently praying over his lifeless body. They declare that God is at work, that His Word is forever true, and that He will not fail them. Every scripture on miracles is being declared and proclaimed over his body.

As time passes, it is evident that Austin is not there, he is gone, and the shell of his body that is left looks nothing like him. His body looks like a picture of sacrifice, of courage, of strength, and of character. Together, with hearts heavy, the family makes the decision that no one should ever have to make, nevertheless, they knew it was time to stop the life support machine. In such a difficult moment, God's peaceful presence began to fill the room. As painful as it was with a hurt that is beyond words, the emptiness and brokenness of hearts was evident, but God was there.   Even with the presence of peace, the words echoed in that room, "My God, My God, My God how can this be?"

Elizabeth was almost to Council Bluffs when she got the call of the plane not making it. This young woman drove from Iowa back to Kansas crying, and praying, not knowing what she was about to experience. She made it to the hospital and Cody met her in the parking lot. Breaking the news to her, she collapsed onto the ground with the sound of a broken heart that was crying out for help. The cries that came from her would make anyone feel the pain she was experiencing. A broken heart and a broken vessel that has lost the love of a good man that cherished her.

Hours have now passed, and it is approaching morning, everyone must say their final good bye and leave to drive home confused, and empty, with no tears left to cry. The Anderson's, once again, are in shock. The Anderson family has had the foundation of their faith shaken again, and a son, so beloved, so young, so full of destiny and purpose lifted from their lives. My God, My God, where are you?

Whether or not a Christian, the first question most people have when facing a loved one's death, is, "God where are you?" It's a natural response and it is more than okay to ask. The Anderson family gets the big picture. We are all living for eternity. The breath we draw here on earth, will not be the breath we draw forever. This is only a temporal place of dwelling, it's not our home. That being said, it is the premature death that we don't understand, nor like. In fact, we hate it. But here the Anderson's find themselves again reminding their hearts that Austin wins.

The truth is, they lose his companionship and the opportunity to watch him walk out his potential here on earth, but Austin wins everything. He receives glory and because of salvation through Christ Jesus, we will see him again! With that truth holding them and giving this family the foundation of hope, even in the midst of this tragedy. It is still difficult to walk out, and they get that. Mary, exemplifying strength, is holding herself, Aubrey and Allie in faith and trust that they will make it again. Papa and Annie are holding themselves together by faith as well, but it so painful for each one of them, as Uncle Cody is planning another funeral service for his family members.

What is different this time is the national news coverage that Austin's story is gaining. The interviews and the phone calls are flooding into the Anderson home. They are all exhausted, making every attempt to grieve. National news affiliates and local stations are coming to the small town of Ringwood, Oklahoma. Local, state, and national newspapers are running the story of the brave Marine who survived the crash, but ultimately, in an attempt to save friends and assist Hannah Luce, lost his battle. *"Greater love hath no man than this, than to lay one's life down for his friend"* (John 15:13 NKJ). Such a true statement that perfectly depicted Austin's death. That is who Austin is. A sacrificial man who gladly stepped up to give his life to help and save others from destruction.

Fox News program Fox and Friends did one of the greatest outlines of images and coverage of the entire story. They invited Cody to join the program live and he was able to share the heart behind the Marine. This story gained so much traction in the news cycle it was shown around the world. The Anderson family received phone calls from Australia, Vietnam, Guatemala, Nicaragua, and Cost Rica in a matter of hours because of the news coverage. The world is looking for brave people and, in this story, Austin captivated them in his last moments on this earth.

Cody makes a phone call to a beautiful church that so freely offers its facility to the Anderson family once again. The Anderson's knew that the funeral service would be large, and to hold the service in the same place that Monte's funeral was held, meant the world to the family. Pastor Wade Burleson of Enid Emmanuel Baptist Church and the staff are some of the most gracious and kindhearted people in Northwest Oklahoma. Their heart and gentleness toward the Anderson family was incredible and so greatly appreciated. A tremendous church full of compassionate people being led by a gifted communicator of the Gospel. The Anderson family cannot express their gratitude enough to Pastor Wade and the staff of Emmanuel.

Another, too familiar, long walk down that aisle once again. Over 2,000 people are in attendance. There are over 100 Freedom Riders outside to pay their respects to this fallen Marine. Austin's Marine Unit from Wichita is present in full military dress. It is a moving sight, but, as these moments often go, wrought with grief and pain. The service is under way, and the faces of the Anderson family are still a reflection of disbelief and pain. Aubrey surrounds his mom with as much strength as he can while Allie sits beside her and Papa. Cody holds on tight to Amy, while on the other side tries his very best to comfort Elizabeth.

The words are comforting, the music soothes, and the video tells a beautiful story of this young life, so full, yet now gone. Ron Luce came and offered comfort and updated the family on Hannah, as she was still in ICU at the time. This looked to be a long road of recovery ahead, but in the end, she will be okay. He is grateful for Austin and celebrated him as a hero. The Anderson family never stopped praying for Hannah's full recovery and restoration. For anyone who has lost a loved one in an accident knows the pain of praying for survivors, while praying for the loss of a loved one is very difficult. Not because we don't want true recovery for the injured, but rather, it forces us to be reminded of the ones who have passed.

At the end of the service, the Marines come forward and take the lead on the recession. They line the aisle of this large church, take Austin's casket and raise it high on their shoulders. They carry this hero out of the service.   You could have heard a pin drop, it was so moving and so heart wrenching at the same time words do not provide any justice to the moment. Looking around the room you see eyes full of tears, and hands covering mouths to holding back the sorrow of this moment. The procession to the cemetery went through the city of Enid, Oklahoma. People lined the streets with flags being held for who is, in their eyes, a great hero. The flashing lights leading this procession lasted for miles.

The Anderson family find themselves pulling into the cemetery and coming to a place that is all too familiar. The burial place of Monte, Austin's father. They will be laid to rest side by side. Lying to rest a son and a grandson is too much for a father and grandfather, mother and grandmother to bear.

To be at this place as a wife and a mother is simply not right. This is beyond fare! To watch Aubrey and Allie look at the grave and see their father, and now older brother being buried, is overwhelming for their already broken hearts. Adding this sorrow to their lives will prove to take a great toll.

It is difficult for most people to drive into a cemetery. One's view of a cemetery is based on their beliefs, their past, and their current convictions. For the Anderson family, they hold to the belief that God is eternal, and He alone has provided a Savior in Jesus Christ. Those who call upon that name, the name of Jesus, and believe that Jesus has risen from the dead, they shall be saved. They shall have eternal life! The belief for this family is that the cemetery is not the final resting place of Austin.   It becomes a place of memorial. This cemetery is a place of remembering and honoring this son, grandson, brother, nephew and friend.

The Anderson's fully understand the difficulty and pain of loss, but it will not define their future. They still have life. Austin's legacy is not to quit, but to live life to the fullest. That is what he embodied. Life! So, they will live life and fulfill God's plan and purpose. They **will** bring beauty out of the ashes. They **will** rise above this moment and honor his memory. Each and every one of us has a past full of adversity, and possibly tragedy. The past does not have to dictate our future. This is the conviction of the Anderson's. "We will give life all we have." This cemetery does not define this family, but it does help us remember the cost, and that life is too short not to live to the fullest.

The grave is not designed to define us that are still living. It is there to present before us our belief, our past to remember the good things, and to build our convictions for this life. Some will go to the cemetery and stare at their past. Without a God centered belief system, you will stare at your past and what is missing with no hope. But with a God centered belief system, you cherish the good and remember what makes you great. Without convictions you start and wonder what could have been. With God centered convictions, you want to live to carry a legacy of what has been put in you by those who have gone on before you. The cemetery is not about death alone, but it is about what is the center of your life. It is about hope, and hope is an anchor to your soul. Hope builds, hope fulfills, and it reveals a love that God has for each, and every one of us.

The Anderson's leave the cemetery carrying broken pieces of their hearts. They will take those pieces and place them on the tapestry of hope and God will heal and God will restore. Just watch!

Out of the Ashes *Chapter 15 –* Out of Control

With head in hands, kneeling at the steps of the stage from which he has released message after message of faith, hope, and God's abundant grace, Pastor Cody Anderson sits in a paralyzed state. Physically, mentally, and spiritually, he is exhausted.

The sanctuary of Faith Center has seen, on many occasions, standing room only crowds. At present time, there are over 400 people that call Faith Center home. This church has been called a miracle in the middle of nowhere.   In a town of less than 200 people, most would call it a country church - and it may be. This small-town church is anything but small. Impacting the region of Northwest Oklahoma and nations like Costa Rica, Nicaragua, Guatemala, Vietnam and Iran. So much vision, so much faith released and trust in the Lord God Almighty. But in this moment, as Cody sits in the sanctuary alone, there is only a crowd of one. Broken and heart full of grief for his family, and the loss of a young man that was like a son. The reality is more than he can bear. Cody stands in the midst of an empty sanctuary and asks God to bring order to the chaos and peace to the storm.

"Things," Cody sighed, "are out of control."

Truly there is nothing that he can do to fix this, or to even offer wisdom to his family.   There is no way to explain how this family could have this unfold again. Words do not exist that could begin to help. With no answers and what seems like a quiet response from heaven, Cody continues to cry out to the living God.

"My heart is empty, I have nothing!" As loud as he could shout it, he releases, "I have nothing!"

Over and over again, that statement rings through the empty sanctuary, as he falls to his knees on the floor, pouring out every drop of emotion left in his heart.   At the end, he rises and says, "God no matter what, I will trust you."

Cody looks up to the ceiling, gives the Lord a nod of his head symbolizing, okay, we will make it. He turns the light out and goes home to Amy and his five children and embraces each one of them, thanking God for what he does have. God then releases an impression upon Cody's heart. That precious impression of the Holy Spirit built an image as real as any video or television screen one has projected. In that image Cody saw the arms of love around Mary, Aubrey, and Allie. It was as if the Lord was saying, "Help me love them." It continued, "Austin and Monte are doing really good, they are with me and I am with you, it will be okay."   It was simple, but things with God are almost always simple. We often complicate them because our minds will not always allow us to see what we need to see. That is why we must walk through moments like this **with** God and not *against* Him. Honestly, we cannot afford to pursue anything less, because anything less, will keep our lives locked into a despair.

Mary, Aubrey, and Allie are in Norman. Mary seems to stay in a state of frustration, and, with all that has been dealt to her, it is not only understandable, but the accepting part of the grieving process. Aubrey begins to turn to alcohol to help deal with the confusion. Pain and emptiness have become too present to deal with from a sober place. The self-medicating is, for at least this moment, creating an illusion of numbing. Sadly, once the fog of alcohol lifts, the reality of hurt is still there.

Allie turns to her friends. Having a full house virtually all the time, she continues to take advantage of alcohol as well. Any opportunity which presented an option to drink, her answer became yes. She would stay busy, but that busy, mixed with alcohol was not a good mix. This family of three is now torn more than ever, confused more than ever and they are searching for any light of hope. But it is hard to see light with blinders on. The enemy uses every chance he can to turn negative experiences into blinders. He has no shortage of tools to use in this family's story.

Aubrey was still drawing a check from the Navy for a few more months and was preparing to use the G I Bill to go back and complete his education. Looking to the future was not something that Aubrey had any interest in. If he could stay numb by drinking alcohol, then he would. Staying away from church was an unspoken goal. It just reminded him of what God has seemingly allowed to happen and taken away from him. He was considering going back to work on the ranch while going to school, but Mary wanted him close to her. He battled with what was next for him. He wanted to be a nearby support for his mother yet had an internal need to pursue a life beyond this current grief and pain.

Allie was turning inwardly, not talking to her mom or anyone in an honest and real way. She wanted to go back to Ringwood and try to hold onto what she could of Austin and her dad, but her mother did not want that. Mary wanted to keep things together and hold them in one place. After all, she already had the other members of her family ripped from her in tragedy. Her attempts, however, were not working. Things were out of control for all of them.

Mary was on the verge of breaking down. She was not feeling good and could not understand what was going on physically. She has always been such a fighter and one who presses through when not feeling well. When she does not feel good for a continued extended time something is wrong. In and out of the hospital emergency room and doctor's appointments, she discovered her heart was having palpitations. Her heart was skipping beats.

The things we would like to skip over are the things that are left unattended. They can be pain, emotional hurt, unforgiveness, and the list can go on and on. Grief is not something that can be skipped over. It is a process of healing that must be attended to. We can't do it alone, and we can't do it hiding from the things that we need to face. When we decide to give the right attention to our grief then sorrow does not hold us. For this wife who has lost her husband and now her oldest son, it is vital to give attention to what is taking place in the heart, both physically and the emotional brokenness. The brokenness of Mary's heart is taking a physical toll on her strength to stand, and her ability to respond. No matter how hard she tries, the energy is not there and the strength at times can be too much of a fight to gain what she needs. Because of the fight in this woman of faith, she determined that she would still be strong for Aubrey and Allie and those close to her.

She is a mom to many, both in love and spiritually. She could be the best encourager, while at the same time making every attempt to try and understand what was going on in her physical body. The struggle was real, but so was her unending faith. What would she do? Everything seems to be out of control.

Every summer, Faith Center hosts a youth summer camp called Elevate Youth Camp. EYC is a gathering of young people to encounter God, His Presence, and His Salvation. Over the years, hundreds of young people have accepted Christ at this camp. It is one of the most powerful things to witness. Cody decided to reach out to Aubrey and ask him to come and help. Aubrey was shocked that Cody asked him to be involved, knowing that Aubrey was not in a good place, and knew about the alcohol problem that was haunting him. Cody was in hope that if Aubrey would just get in the right atmosphere, then God could shift his focus off of the pain.

As someone who has worked with many people in rough seasons of life, Cody understands that you can't replace something with nothing. If the something that Aubrey was dealing with was pain, and the symptom was alcohol abuse, then the pain must be replaced with healing so that the symptom can be peace and clarity. This was the something Cody could offer, so he did. Aubrey accepted the offer. He came and served and did an incredible job for his uncle but what happened to Aubrey was nothing short of a miracle.

There was an afternoon that Cody was alone taking a break and beginning to prepare for the night service. Aubrey came into where Cody was, and they just talked. About an hour into it, Cody asked Aubrey if he was the only one who had ever lost somebody. Aubrey answered with a no. Cody then leaned into the conversation and said,

"Then stop acting like you are the only one in the world who has lost someone."

Aubrey began to think about that and God was starting a process in Aubrey that would change his life forever.

The next day, Cody spoke a message surrounding Austin's story. It had a gripping effect on Aubrey. In the message, with Austin's photo on the screens, Cody made a statement that the Holy Spirit used to penetrate the heart of this young man.

"There are millions of people who lose their life every day, and yes God is there. He is there to comfort, He is there to help. We are not alone, but if we are still on this earth, then we need to pick up the mantle of those that we love and keep carrying the message, keep living in hope, and trust in God."

That day, stage right, was a young man with his hands lifted up to a loving God, and by the Holy Spirit, Aubrey began to break. As he broke, God took the pieces of what was broken and began to put them back together. The blinders the enemy had placed on him were removed.

The miracle is this, he sensed God at work in his life. He had been angry and mad at God for taking from him. In a moment, that all changed, and he experienced God as a giver. The desire for alcohol left him in that experience and he did not have another drink from that day forward. What a miracle!

The atmosphere for healing is awaiting you. I don't know if it is at a church service like Aubrey found, or if it is somewhere else. You must get out of the trap of the lie that says, "God is a taker and not a giver." Everything changed for Aubrey that day and God began to do a work in him that changed his life forever. For what was unfolding, he needed that moment! For Aubrey, things were starting to make sense and where he was out of control, he started allowing God to be in control. He started to trust again.

It is now August and Allie continues to fight with the landscape of life. The parties are getting out of hand. She used to be able to call Austin, but Austin was no longer there.   Aubrey had decided to work closer to Ringwood and attend classes at Northern Oklahoma College. He wanted to be involved at Faith Center, so he moved in with Papa and Annie at the ranch. His role was to help Papa on the weekends. Allie wanted to be back home and to attend church at Faith Center as well, but neither one of them wanted to leave their mother alone. Mary could not stand for her children to be away from her. She did understand the draw to Faith Center, and to be closer to what was familiar for them. It was very frustrating for her to not be able to provide that for Allie.

For Allie, things were far out of control. There was no one listening to her, even though people were around her that cared, her statements were being poured out on empty ears. If you asked people around her at the time, they would each tell you that she never talked about it, but, an important lesson of life teaches that people speak volumes in their silence. She was being ear damaging silent. She had plenty to say, yet, no one seemed to hear.   Something needed to change, something needed to give.   Allie had no idea what that was.

She decided to go to the opening football game of Norman North, where she attended High School. It was the beginning of her Senior year. Her and some friends met earlier and had a few too many drinks before the ballgame. It was recognized that she had too much to drink, and in just a moments time, Allie found herself in a desperate moment.

A police officer arrests Allie for public intoxication. She is under age and this is as low as a moment for Allie than what she had ever experienced in her young life. She was embarrassed, disappointed in herself, and utterly confused. As she sits in the back of that squad car with the lights flashing, she has an image that awakened her heart. God specializes in moments where we never expect Him to show up.

The truth is, He is always there. That is why the Word of God declares, *"I will never leave nor forsake you,"* Hebrews 13:5.   God will use every possible moment to get your attention. As He gets it, you lift your eyes from yourself and unto Him. Everything can change. It is hard to explain, but it happens.   Are you willing to see Him more than you see yourself?

Allie looks through the lights that are flashing and she immediately sees herself. Not just the current self, but she catches the glimpse of when she was 5 years old sitting in the back of her mother's car, seeing the lights flash at her dad's accident. She sees the little girl, crying because all she wanted was to see her dad and she could not. In that moment, she cried out to God and asked for help and said out loud, "I just want to go home." Mary makes the drive and comes to pick up Allie. She is out of responses and does not know what to do. Allie told her mom late in the night, "I just want to go home to Ringwood. I want to go to where I feel home, where I feel dad and I feel Austin.   When I am at home, I see them, and I want that. Can I just go home?"

Mary knows that something is not right within her heart, but no one can tell her what is going on. She does not want to feel what she is feeling, but just can't get a hold of what is wrong. The truth is everything is wrong! Everything is out of control! She has lost her husband and now her oldest son. Her heart is broken spiritually, emotionally and physically. She does not know what to do, but she knows she needs to do something. Something needs to shift for multiple reasons. Mary begins to cry. In the rocking recliner in the living room of her home, she sits. Crying out to God with so much desperation she asks God to take the confusion, take the pain, take the impossible, help! It was a very difficult decision to let Allie finish her senior year at Ringwood.   Mary wanted to be away from the memories.

The multiple disagreements with the Anderson family throughout the years did not help. Everyone's intentions were for what they thought was right. Frustrations against what each other had thought was wrong rose to the forefront many times. Everyone wanted the best for the kids and for Mary.   Mary did not always agree with Cody and with Don and Carrol Ann. There were many moments that were ugly on the surface. Not every conversation ended well, and feelings were hurt. Cuts into the fiber of relationships, had ranged from minor scrapes to near amputations. Truth reveals that, when you have so much loss and brokenness people are going to get hurt.

It was breaking Mary's heart even more to go back to Ringwood and let Allie do this, but, reluctantly, that was what she decided to do. Allie steps out of her mother's vehicle and takes her bags into Annie and Papa's house. The peacefulness of the ranch and attending the school she started in kindergarten and was now returning as a senior in high school. This seemed right to Allie. Agreements are made with Don, Carrol Ann, and Mary with Cody helping as well. This would be good for Allie and everyone involved was committed to her success and begin this process of restoration in relationships and helping one another. Even though it was very difficult, because of that commitment, there was a peace in this decision.

Something supernatural happened in the back of that police car for Allie. God met with her in that moment. He gave her an image that she lifted her eyes and she began to see hope. She caught a glimpse of what it looked like to become healed, as well as the steps that needed to be taken to restore herself.   Allie knew what she needed to do next. From that moment Allie left the pursuit of alcohol, never to return to that scene of life again. Everything changed that night, because God was at work, protecting her and establishing a faith that could handle the storm that she was in, and the one that was about to unfold.

Mary drives down the long driveway of Anderson Ranch. Her heart is so broken as she drives back home to Norman by herself. Alone. What she has felt on the inside has manifested to the external. She is alone. Tears feel her eyes as she drives away, because she knows that something is not right. But at least Allie will be where she needs to be. Mary will never make it down that driveway again, but in this moment, she knows that Allie is okay and that is the most important thing. Out of control, but with an unconditional love, Mary loves her children as she prepares for the greatest battle of her life.

Out of the Ashes *Chapter16* – The Heart Matters

We've all heard the phrase "a lot of heart." It is a term we use to describe someone's drive and tenacity, in a positive way. The reason we use "heart" as a reference for strength is because there is no other organ or muscle in the human body, that if it were to stop functioning, the rest of the body simply shuts down and dies. It is the strongest point of reference we can comprehend. The heart is very unique to say the least. This one organ carries the load in providing all the necessities of operation in the intricate detail of the human body. In fact, even in biblical terms, the importance that God places on the heart is revealed through His word. The heart of man is mentioned over 900 times in the Bible. Proverbs 4:23 says, *"Guard your heart with all diligence, for out of it spring the issues of life."*

As just mentioned, moments ago, without the heart working at its fullest potential other organs will fail and life is unable to sustain. When the heart does its job in pumping blood to the various organs, the brain receives oxygen, and all is well. Muscles need oxygen, glucose and amino acids, as well as the proper ratio of sodium, potassium, and salts in order to contract normally. Without the heart, all these functions would fail. Essentially, if the heart was to fail, the entire body would shut down in a matter of minutes. This is why everyday matters. This is why the moments that we are afforded in this life must receive our best. Our best in love! Our best in faith! Our best in time!

The truth is, time is one of the few things we can never recapture. We don't always get the moment to take the words that have been spoken and get them back. When we do, it is most often like trying to unscramble an egg. Even more importantly, we don't get the moments back to share what is on our heart. We say it often, "All we have is time on our side." Or, how about this one, "I will have time to get to that later." We can't get time back, ask any elder. Time is shorter than what we think. We are not promised another tomorrow.

Thank God for his divine grace on the time we do have, because without it, we may miss the precious opportunities that stand before us. Once we pass from this physical realm into the eternal spiritual realm, we will never have the chances to influence others the way we do right now. While, for those of us who are Christ followers, we do have a promise to spend eternity together, the truth is, many will not make it there with us. God relies on His people utilizing the time we have on this earth to reach others for Him. Once this is gone, never again will we have the moments at work, at the gas station, at the school or anywhere else our regular patterns take us past the people God has entrusted into our care. Time is precious, non-refundable, non-transferable and short.

Mary's time was getting shorter. With each day, her heart was becoming weaker and weaker. From the outside perspective, with all she had been through, how could it not. Sadly, this physical condition was just another weight being piled on top of her strong, but tired shoulders. Doctors suggested that she could have received some type of infection earlier while on a mission's trip to Central America that may have affected her heart. There was also the possibility that its origin derived from an infection produced by a dental procedure in her past. How she arrived at this point was surrounded by many thoughts and possibilities, and even more questions. What mattered in this moment was that something needed to be done.

Mary's doctors told her that her heart was failing. She needed to be put on the heart transplant list and it was her only hope of surviving. They put her in a "Life" vest that would shock her if her heart was to stop. Mary was able to go home where she could be comfortable. She could not work, she could not exert energy, and could not lift anything. Mary's sisters and other friends came to stay with her to make sure she was okay. Aubrey and Allie would come and see her around their school class times and work schedule.

Mary was so very tired and weak. She had buried her son Austin just months earlier. Her husband was only within reach through memory. She was full of fear and disbelief of what was facing her, and the new battle that life was presenting to her. For her kids, she would be strong. For them she would show tremendous faith. Mary was a person that would always defy the odds.   She had always stepped up against difficulties and overcame. That is who she is. Now, in this moment, it would take an effort that is beyond comprehension. There was a battle to walk through.

Mary had "O" negative blood, and the chances of finding a transplant with "O" negative blood was within the 2 percent range. The odds of survival are not high, but you would not tell Mary Anderson that. She could fight these odds and make it. Her confession was strong, and her faith was continuing to build each and every day.

Days later, Mary starts to retain major amounts of fluid. Her sister, Donna takes her to Integris Heart Hospital and they admit her into the Intensive Care Unit. It is there that a specialist makes a decisive move to put a pump system on one chamber of Mary's heart. This pump system basically does for the heart what it is unable to do for itself. The surgical staff moves Mary up the list for transplant. Once again, this entire family is believing for a miracle.   Aubrey, who just months ago had a wall built in his heart against God, is now praying and standing for a miracle. Allie, who just weeks ago was angry at life and not in a place where she wanted to be, is trusting in God for a miracle.

Mary's sisters and friends are taking turns staying with Mary in the hospital. You could see the love and support from so many flooding into the hospital. Everyone is waiting for the call that a transplant is ready. But then, more bad news comes to Mary. The other chamber of her heart is weakening. Without a transplant she would not survive, and the only option is to put a second pump system on the other chamber of her heart. Within weeks, Mary has gone from walking, standing and doing life, to being in Intensive Care with two heart pump systems making her heart work. This is the new norm for Mary, though her skin is not burned, and her brain is functioning, much like her first son in his last moments on earth, machines are keeping her alive.

All around the room, cards and scriptures that she is standing on fill the walls.   There are a tremendous number of friends that are there showing support to her. Aubrey and Allie are coming as much as possible. Mary's sisters were doing everything they could to show support, prayer and help. Cody came to visit and pray with Mary every chance he got.

When you prayed with Mary, she would grasp your hand very tight.   She was holding onto faith, holding on to prayer and holding onto her trust in God.   A miracle had to happen, and Mary knew that all too well. There is a scurry in the room by the staff of nurses. The announcement is made, "Mary, we have a match and we are going to need to prep you immediately for transplant surgery." There is not much expression on Mary's face. The thought of someone else's heart beating inside you was a very difficult thing to grasp. Mary would say often, "I just desire for God to heal my heart, because I don't want to see someone else lose their life, just so I can be helped."

Mary was the one who always helped, the one who would always sacrifice.   If Mary could sacrifice anything of her own, she would for anyone that she cared about.

Mary is at this place, in this moment realizing that if this does not work, her life will end. The preparation for heart transplant is a grueling process. The transplant surgery is one of the most complex and strenuous procedures that the human body can withstand. With each transplant, the surgeons have to be positive that the heart will take with the specific blood type and that it will function like it is supposed to. Mary is surgically prepped, and everyone is nervous, understanding the importance of this procedure having to work. The surgeons test the new heart in multiple ways to assure that it will be the match that they need. Mary is expecting to wake up with a functioning heart at work on the inside of her.

In the waiting room is family. Mary's mother, her sisters, and many other members are there. Cody, Aubrey, and Allie along with close friends, are believing for a miracle. There is not one person who cares deeply about Mary that is not in prayer and trusting in God for a miracle. The bible says in Proverbs 3 to *"Trust in the Lord with all your heart and lean not on your own understanding." (Proverbs 3:5 NKJ) Trust* is the reality of your faith at work. When someone is able to trust in God, even though the circumstances are saying something different, and we don't understand it, we still trust in God.

This a moment of faith for the entire family. This must work! We don't understand what and why we are walking through this right now, but we lean not on our own understanding, but trust in God. What do you trust in? Where does your faith rest? Aubrey and Allie and everyone close to Mary is leaning on God, trusting in Him. But that trust and faith is about to be shaken once more.

The surgeon comes to visit with the family. He informs the family that the heart would not be the perfect match for Mary and the second person on the transplant list received the heart. Mary was in the recovery process for a long time and was unable to talk because of the tube helping her breathe. The pump system was still pumping both chambers of her heart. When she woke up, someone would have to tell her that it did not work. The tears begin to flow, and the level of fear began to rise. Mary is put back at the top of the transplant list and would have to recover for a few days from the procedure. Once again, Mary would have to wait it out.

Mary continued to fight, but her heart was so weak, and the pump systems were not designed to work for a long period of time. Time was running out without a miracle. So many people and ministries came to pray for Mary. Mary would do what no other person had attempted to do. She would have the nursing staff, many times with Aubrey assisting as well, take her for walks. She would walk while the staff would push the pump systems. They would take up the whole hall way and make a round. Mary would walk, she would fight, she would stand in prayer, but each day she was getting weaker.

While Aubrey sat alongside her bed, a doctor came into the room. She was resting as he began to strike up a conversation with Aubrey. He was inquisitive of what Aubrey was doing and how he was doing. The conversation began to extend to where Aubrey shared with the doctor about the loss of his father, and his older brother, and now, with much emotion behind his words, facing the impossible with his mother.

The doctor replied to Aubrey, "As active as your mother was, the walking and running, all the things that she did, should have produced a healthy heart. Your mom has been through so much in her life, that literally she is dying of a broken heart."

Those words from that doctor shook Aubrey to the core. He began to think to himself about how true that could be. She lost the love of her life. Both of her boys moved out of the house to live with their grandparents. Mary always struggled with that decision and at times there was a wall between her and Monte's parents. Mary wasn't mad at them, but the situation, the process, the choices that were made, it all added up to be painful.   Then with Austin's horrific accident, she was hurting, and she was feeling alone.

"Could all of this be why her heart was so empty and unhealthy?" Aubrey thought to himself, "What if she is holding on to certain things that she needs to forgive?"

Aubrey remembers what he just went through a few months back, the decision to let go, and the decision to forgive himself, to forgive his dad for leaving, amongst other things. Because of what he had just gone through, he wondered if his mother, this woman of such strength that is battling for her life, needs to let go of some things, to forgive and be at peace. He did not know what to do or what to think about all these thoughts running through his mind. One thing he did know, if there was anything at all that he could do to help his mother in any way, he wanted to do it.

Close to three months have gone by. Mary would say, over and over again, "It is in God's Hands." She loved the staff of the ICU. Even in her weak moments, she would lighten the mood and make people laugh. She would take a syringe, fill it full of water out of her cup, and shoot water at the staff. They would laugh with her and she with them. They loved Mary! What an incredible team of people, nurses, and doctors. They would help, they would serve, and do everything they possible could to make Mary comfortable.

Then, abruptly and suddenly, the nurses rush in and the frantic movement of machines and preparation begins. They have found another match and Mary would need to be ready for another procedure if everything matched. She was so tired, the look in her eyes telling the story of what she was feeling. It is the same picture in the waiting room again. Friends and family are there, all waiting for the call from the surgeon. Again, all the procedural steps are complete, and Mary is wheeled into the operating room awaiting a new heart. This has to be it! This has to take place! The surgeon calls and talks to the family. And in a disappointing turn, the second attempt is the same as the first.   The heart went to the second person on the transplant list.   Mary is still in recovery and will awake without a new heart, having to face the fight once again. This hit the family like a ton of bricks. When Mary is informed that it did not work, tears flowed down her cheeks. Once again, she could not speak because of the tube in her throat. Until she could breathe on her own the tube had to stay. Everyone is heartbroken. The wind is out of their sails and the kid's faith has been battered as they stand for a miracle of their mom.

A few days later Mary makes the determination to exercise and work harder.   The rest of her body was functioning very well. The doctors told her that if she worked to get to a certain point, there was a larger machine that she could transfer to that would do the job of the current two. If she continued to get strong enough there was another pump system that she could take home. With this information given to her, Mary went to work. Oklahoma News stations came to do a story on Mary. There has not been anyone to take two heart pump systems as far as she has. No one has physically walked and became better on these systems.   She was determined that God did not want to give her a new heart but to heal the one she has. With determination she continued to do what she could.

There were days where Mary's determination was strong, and there were days where it was low. Mary's room was empty, aside from Cody, who was visiting. It was very difficult in those moments. "I am scared of what may happen." Mary said with tears coming down her face.

"God is able to move in our lives at a given moment." Cody would encourage Mary.

Mary asked, "What do I need to do, I have done it all, I just don't know anymore."

Cody responded, "It is not just about doing, it is about being."

He continued, "Be, a daughter of God. Be a person of faith, just be and allow God to be who He is, love and strength and peace to you. Mary, we don't always understand the journey, but God has you and He is with you!"

"I am so mad at Monte for leaving me, I am mad that Austin is gone, I am mad that I am here in this condition." Mary cried.

"You have every right to be mad and to be confused about all this." Cody continued, "Let's do this, let's just pray and forgive them for leaving and let's ask God to forgive us for being angry and even ask Him to forgive us for being angry at Him." Cody finished by saying, "When there is forgiveness, healing comes to our emotions, and even to our very heart and body. Do you want to do this?" Cody asked.

With her head down and her eyes closed she prays and then stops. "It is too hard for me to do all of this and to forgive those that I need to forgive, but I know I need to." Mary said. She prays more and as Cody is holding her hand, she grips even tighter and asks for Cody to pray over her.

Over and over again Cody repeats, "May your peace come, O God let your peace flood this place, this body and this heart." Mary fell asleep, and there was peace in the room and over her. It is amazing what prayer can do, even when the situation looks so terrible. Trust in God and lean not on your own understanding.

Why would this subject of forgiveness surface so much? Is it because we all needed to be reminded of what unforgiveness produces? Unforgiveness is like drinking poison and hoping that someone else will die. It is a prison to our emotions and a blockade against God. Jesus said this: *"If you cannot forgive your brother, then your Father in Heaven will not forgive you"*. Enough said! Forgiveness is freedom, and liberty, and a key to our spiritual and emotional health. Where forgiveness flows, love can and will freely flow. We don't have time to hold things in, or to hold things against other people. If there is anything that the Anderson family understands it is this: "Life is short, and you don't always have tomorrow."

Even though Mary's strength was weak, and her faith was being challenged, she would pursue peace and continue to lean into God. Mary would continue to have conversations with Aubrey.

"Aubrey, I can't leave you alone, if I am gone you and Allie will be all alone," said Mary.

Aubrey replied, "Mom you have taken care of us, sacrificed for us, you need to take care and do what is best for you." Aubrey continued, "Allie will be fine, she is surrounded by more than enough people and I will make sure she is taken care of."

"I am torn between what is here and what is there," Mary said. "I love both places, one is Austin and your dad, and the other is you and Allie. I don't know what is going to take place. I see heaven and I am scared of what I see here." Mary cried.

The tears in that hospital were beyond any description of words or images. It was so difficult. Every day would be up and then down for Mary. No one knew what the next day was going to bring. Mary was too well to be in ICU, but she had too many needs to go to a regular floor room.   Everyone thought she was getting better, but in a moments time, everything changed.

She started retaining too much fluid and the pump system was not doing what the natural system needed. There was no sign of a possible donor and time was running out. Out of nowhere, Aubrey receives a phone call.

"Aubrey, get to the hospital. The doctors are saying that your mother does not have much time." Donna said.

Donna is Mary's older sister and was so dedicated to being there at every turn and every moment that she possibly could. For six months, this hospital has not only been home to Mary, but to Donna as well. Mary's other sisters did everything they could to help. Good friends like Brenda Botts and Haley Gualey spent hours and hours at the hospital.

Aubrey called Cody and he brought Allie to the city, not knowing what to expect. They had been in this place multiple times before. They are both afraid of what may be waiting for them. When Cody and Allie arrive at the hospital, they go to the main elevators and meet the family in the waiting room. The hallway outside of Mary's room was full of people. Allie goes in to the room, Aubrey is already there standing beside the bed holding his mother's hand. Aubrey looks at his sister and then looks away, Allie begins to cry as she approaches the bedside of her mother. Following the first heart transplant that failed, Mary decided at that point she did not want anyone to have to make any more difficult decisions than what were necessary, so she signed a Do Not Resuscitate order. Mary's broken heart was no longer able to function on its own. As many people as allowed went into the room to say good bye to this hero. The fight had come to an end, the pump system off, and with a last breath Mary Anderson, friend of friends, champion of faith, overcomer of obstacles and lover of people, daughter of the Most High God, steps into the embrace of her Savior.

Aubrey and Allie embrace one another and here they stand alone, afraid and broken. Aubrey comes out of the room to gather his thoughts and upon turning the corner, the weight of everything that just happened came crashing down and he collapsed in the hallway.

Monte, Austin and now Mary all gone. How do you deal with that? How do you even have conversation about that? What else could this family face? The answer to that is simple. They could face nothing else, there is nothing worse in this world than facing death and the loss of loved ones like these two have had to do. It does not make any sense. It is not even fair! But there is a difference.

That day was another day of brokenness. The testimony of Aubrey and Allie is that there was a peace over that day, the broken heart of their mother was healed, and they knew she was in the place of miracles. The heavens have opened up and she is not afraid anymore, she is not lonely anymore, she does not have to cry one more tear. She is healed! They knew that, and that is the peace that they hold onto.

Aubrey is immediately faced with a load of responsibility. His mother's hospital bills, planning her funeral and much, much more. Allie once again feels alone even with those who are around her. There would be no more conversations, the laugh of her mother would no longer be a sound that her ears got to absorb. A daughter without a father, and now without a mother. If one ever doubted the Grace of God in the midst of tragedy, then they just have to look at Allie and Aubrey Anderson and see that what God had done in them months before in preparing their hearts for this moment. God is always walking with us, and His Grace is always moving on our behalf. We don't understand it. We will not ever get it as far as the question "why?" But knowing He is there and knowing He loves us enough to prepare for what is ahead, helps make us secure when things are unstable.

Once again, Emmanuel Baptist Church is called upon to host a funeral for this family. The service was beautiful and so honoring of Mary Francis Anderson, a woman who sacrificed so much in the midst of loss, a woman whose testimony is heroic for her efforts to survive and fight. If ever there were a person with "a lot of heart." it was Mary Anderson.

Out of the Ashes *Chapter 17 – Out of the Ashes*

Tragedy and crisis strike at the heart of millions of families every day. It can come in various forms. Abuse, abandonment, death, critical illness, catastrophic events and all else you want to name. The stress of these events can cause even the strongest people emotionally, spiritually, and sometimes even physically to be burned out. It is in times like these, we must rely on the fact that, no matter how much the fire rages or the intensity of the crisis, there is always a way through. Nowhere in the Bible does it tell us that we will not experience difficult things. In fact, the Word of God prepares us for trials of fire, for moments of crisis and tragedy. John 16:33 declares, *"These things I have spoken to you, that in Me you may have peace. In the world you will have tribulation; but be of good cheer, I have overcome the world."* (John 16:33 NKJ) James 1:2 - 4 it says, *"My brethren, count it all joy when you fall into various trials, knowing that the testing of your faith produces patience. But let patience have its perfect work, that you may be perfect and complete, lacking nothing."*

(James 1:2-4 NKJ)

We have mentioned throughout this story that the world is broken and in a broken world things, people, and families will be broken. The fires will rage against us at some point. We will all be faced with challenges to our life, our belief system, and character. The question is, will **we** rise out of the ashes of defeat?   One of many powerful scriptures that was foundational for the Anderson family is found in Daniel 3:27.

It's the story of three Hebrew children who would not bow down to worship a false God. King Nebuchadnezzar commanded that these three young men be thrown into the fire. As the King looked into the furnace, he did not see three shadows, but he saw a fourth and the fourth image was the Son of God in the midst of the fire. When they came out, there was no smell of smoke upon them.   Daniel 3:27

says, "*And the satraps, administrators, governors, and the king's counselors gathered together, and they saw these men on whose bodies the fire had no power; the hair of their head was not singed nor were their garments affected, and the smell of fire was not on them.*" (Daniel 3:27 NKJ) They went through the fire, and out of the ashes they came.

There was not the smell of fire on them.

For the Anderson's, they have gone through the fire and they do not forget the pain of the journey. They remember that God is with them and the smell of the fire is not present. They still trust with all their heart, the goodness of God. When you can see God in the fire and trust that He will deliver you, no matter what it looks like around you, He is able to deliver! He **is** able to comfort! He **is** able to restore! In that same fire, Jesus stood with the three young men. Prior to them being forced into the fiery furnace these young men said, "...even the God we serve will deliver us out of the fiery furnace." They came out of the fire and out of the ashes of what was designed to defeat them and stood, because God delivered them. They made a shift. Friends it is simple, in the fire look to Jesus and He will deliver.   We don't always know what that deliverance looks like, but God has us.

For Monte, H.O. Austin and Mary their deliverance was straight into the arms of Jesus. Eternally whole and complete. What a beautiful thing. For the Anderson family that deliverance is restored faith and the "new" that God is providing. It is not easy, but we have risen out of the ashes with the sweet-smelling aroma of God's Grace and not the smell of fire that was designed to defeat us. We triumph in Christ Jesus and we look for tomorrow.

Today, "Out of the Ashes," Dedria is remarried to a wonderful man who has been a God send to her following the loss of H.O. Robert Bryan, Dedria, and their son Caleb still live in East Texas, loving life and doing well.   Dedria's two children, Whitney and Heston are doing very well. Whitney lives with her son Triston in Ringwood, Oklahoma. Whitney is a care giver and working hard to provide for her son every day. Heston is married to Kara and both served in the Navy, and now live in Gulf Port Mississippi. They have a daughter named Cheyanne.

Today, "Out of the Ashes," Aubrey is married to Jordyn. They live in Enid, Oklahoma and serve on staff as pastors at Faith Center. They first met at EYC summer camp, then one year later, Aubrey proposed to Jordyn on the stage of EYC and she said yes. They are expecting their first child. It is a boy and his name will be Grey Anderson.

Today, "Out of the Ashes," Allie is married to Kolton Johnson. They live in Stillwater and will be completing their bachelor's degrees there. They love to serve God in any way possible and are doing incredible with the future looking very bright.

Today, "Out of the Ashes," The Anderson family is serving God with all their hearts. They are willing to **go**, willing to **be,** and willing to **do** whatever needs to be done to propagate the Gospel of Jesus Christ in the region of Northwest Oklahoma.

Cody and Amy have five children, Abigail, Alexa, Alec, Adam and Ayven. They love God and are filled with passion to worship and serve people in any way possible. Faith Center Fellowship is extending itself to be a church with three locations in Northwest Oklahoma. God is amazing, and if we are willing to look unto Him in the midst of the fire, we will come through not smelling like fire, and out of the ashes we will rise.

In the upcoming chapters we will take you through five foundational steps that are critical to seeing through the fire and place your attention on Jesus. He is there, and He alone will deliver you through. You may not know how, and it may not look like anything you have imagined in your own mind, but in the end it will be good. For God is a good, good God!   **The five critical steps are:**

1. **Answering the question, "What Now?"** We must put God where He belongs in the lens of your life.   You have to know where He is in the midst of the tragedy, storm, or crisis. He is there. Can you see Him?

2.   **Recognize the enemy of restoration.**   The enemy
comes to steal, kill and destroy.   Grief is not just a
journey, but a road block. We must recognize that there is
a healthy journey to restoration, but we must avoid the
road block.

3.   **Walk in the peace of God.**   Peace is not just a saying,
but it is a powerful force from God that is at work to
sustain you and hold you in the place of restoration.

4.   **How to move forward.**   The Word of God is very
clear for those who have endured loss. There is a way to
move forward from where you are. God has a purpose
and you and I must walk that purpose out.

5.   **Overwhelmed by Grace.**   In the midst of our loss,
God is moving, and He is moving on our behalf causing His
divine Grace to abound in the midst of our circumstances.
We are in charge of our own faith and we cannot allow
loss, tragedy and above all, grief lock us away to where we
are unable to see God's Amazing Grace.

Each of these foundational steps will help you in the midst of
what seems like fire. When it seems like it will be the end of you and
there is no hope, God will not leave you abandoned or alone. He is
constantly at work on your behalf. Take the steps necessary and
repeat them over and over again, and you will rise out of the ashes.

Denial, anger, bargaining, depression and acceptance, these are what the majority of psychologists and counselors believe to be the 5 stages of grief. Some say there are seven stages and have included what is called the "Upward Trend" and "Reconstruction." The truth is, as we have stated multiple times throughout the book: "Everyone deals with grief differently". Even though that is true, there are always basic strides one must take to not allow a *spirit of grief* that keeps you from grieving in a healthy way. We should all desire to stay in a place of healing and restoration. What we have recognized in helping people walk through their loss, separation in family and/ or tragedy, is that a cornerstone hurdle that one must face is the question of "What Now?"

This question comes into play very quickly in the midst of loss. Its visit becomes a regularity.   Even after immediate decisions have been made there will be another "What Now?" Six months down the road will introduce another, "What Now?" One year later and then two years later will be another "What Now?" If that question continually arises in our pathway to restoration and healing, we need to deal with it. While "I don't know" may be the true answer, it will not prove effective long-term. Please understand, on the onset of dealing with that cornerstone question, it is okay to respond with "I don't know." It really is okay. Just don't allow yourself to stay in the place of always responding that way.

If a person stays in a place emotionally, mentally and even physically of always saying "I don't know" then confusion is setting in. Where confusion stays as a prevalent state of mind, the spirit of grief influences one's heart and attitude to not change. It is aiding in the thought pattern to stay trapped in a framework of defeat and grief. We must overcome those moments by the Word of God and His presence touching those areas. With that perspective and truth being revealed, our eyes can be opened to what needs to be done.

The first step is being realistic and honest about where we really are, but further steps require catching a vision to not stay in that state. Without vision, people perish, and vision requires clarity. To explain biblically why we need to face this and overcome confusion is vitally important in stepping toward healing and restoration. The Bible explains the source of confusion in **1 Corinthians 14:33 (NKJ)** *"For God is not the author of confusion but of peace, as in all the churches of the saints."*

Please notice that the author of confusion is not God but of the enemy. Some may say, "but wait a minute, there were times under the old covenant that God used confusion upon Israel's enemies." That is true, but the confusion was because of their disobedience and the position as enemies of God. The bottom line is this: God is author of life and He will not script confusion for you to live in the rest of your life. **James 3:16 (NKJ)** says *"For where envy and self-seeking exist, confusion and every evil thing are there."* Notice that confusion and every evil thing is there. Why is that? Because God is not authoring confusion in your life, it is the enemy against your restoration. The enemy is the spirit of grief at work against your healing and the ability to find joy in the midst of your sorrow.

I like to put it this way: Confusion is the enemy's playground leading one into deception. Being deceived that one is unable to cope, or that someone is unable to move from where they are without the one who is gone. Again, that is all natural to feel that way and hold those types of thoughts and emotions. We just can't stay there. To camp out in the land of confusion will open the door to the wrong author of your future and the wrong pattern of thinking. You will quickly find yourself becoming a citizen of a land you were only supposed to journey through. The taxes in such a place will empty out the already drained resources left from trauma.

Another word for confusion in the bible is the word "dismayed." Look at what instructions come to Joshua amid his life. Moses is dead and Joshua, the servant of the Lord, is now taking the lead. God instructs him in **Joshua 1:9 (NKJ)** *"Have I not commanded you? Be strong and of good courage; do not be afraid, nor be dismayed, for the Lord your God is with you wherever you go."* Be strong! Be courageous! Do not be dismayed or confused. Why? God is with you wherever you go. When you are in the midst of dealing with loss the last thing you want to hear is be strong, take courage. I know. I have been there, but my friend please hear me out, it is not just me telling you this, it's the very Word of God speaking to you and saying, be strong! You and I do not have to walk around being led by the **wrong** author of our next step. Our next step is coming to the place where we realize that God **is** with us! That is right! What now Lord? You are with us! It is the starting point of a new journey and a foundation to build within our restoration.

Right now, ask yourself the question: Who is my author? In case you are too weakened at the moment, let me help you answer. It is God! Confusion and being dismayed will NOT hold you back from healing and restoration.   Prior to verse nine of Joshua chapter one is an outline that every Christian should place within the discipline of their faith when facing death, crisis, and turmoil. **Joshua 1:7-8 (NKJ)**

*"Only be **strong** and **very courageous**, that you may observe to do according to all the law which Moses My servant commanded you; do not turn from it to the right hand or to the left, that you may prosper wherever you go. 8 This Book of the Law shall not depart from your mouth, but you shall meditate on it day and night, that you may observe to do according to all that is written in it. For then you will make your way prosperous, and then you will have good success."*

Observe the fact we must live our life according to God's Word and His Will for my life, not to turn from it at all. We are to meditate in the Word of God and then our way will be made successful. You change who the author of your healing is when you mediate on the right things. Meditate on the Word and Promises of the Almighty. Take captive the right thoughts and God will script and author your healing.   The Bible declares in **2 Corinthians 10:5 (NKJ)** *"casting down arguments and every high thing that exalts itself against the knowledge of God, bringing every thought into captivity to the obedience of Christ,"* When we take the wrong thoughts that are being authored by a spirit of grief and bring them unto the obedience or meditation of God's Word, we will overcome! It will happen, God's Word produces incredible fruit in our thought life.

Right now, ask yourself the question, "Who is my author?" "Who am I listening to?" In order to overcome confusion, we must take captive the wrong thoughts and establish the right pattern of thinking, according to the Word of God. This is critical to us because if we do not recognize this, it will lead to depression. Depression is a trap by the enemy to keep one locked into a spiraling thought process that says nothing is going to change. Again, I contend my friend, that if depression is starting to appear, you have begun to listen to the wrong author. If depression is setting in, you must face it and change the author of your restoration. God is there! Meditate on His Word and watch the meditation of your heart speak to the areas of your life where you need healing. I am going to come back to this term meditation in a moment, but before I do let's take a close look at the stages of depression.

Stages of depression:

1. **Overwhelming and extended sadness.**
There are a number of things that can cause one to be sad. Obviously, loss of a loved one or another traumatic event can extend our sadness. The key is to look at the extension of our sadness. The Bible says that sorrow will last for a night, but joy comes in the morning. Now this does not mean that we should expect people to get over it quickly, but it should not be for an extended period of time. If it is, then we are allowing the author of confusion, dismay, and depression script for us something that will keep us away from healing and restoration. How long is to long? No one can put a specific time frame on this subject. However, if you are sitting there three years down the road still being burdened by sadness then, my friend, you are in a state of depression, and the wrong author is scripting your thoughts.

2. **Feeling of daily fatigue.**
It is the place where one will feel exhausted and extreme weariness. If this is a daily issue, then we must confront the wrong author, begin to heal and be restored. Fatigue is not only feeling tired and exhausted, but it is not having the energy to work or to face the problems of the day. At any

point when a person is done facing problems and they are full of fatigue then they are on the verge of being fully depressed.

3.   Insomnia.

When you can't sleep, something is not in order. Rest is a healer to our emotions and rest is where we refuel our lives. If there is an absence of rest, we are naturally tired, full of fatigue, and just exhausted. We must sleep and sleep well to receive healing to our body and our emotions. This is not just a physical rest, it is also what changes the author of depression from speaking to your thoughts. It opens up the door to rest in God's peace.

Look at what the Bible says in **Matthew 28:11- 10 (NKJ)**
"Come to Me, all you who labor and are heavy laden, and I will give you rest. 29 Take My yoke upon you and learn from Me, for I am gentle and lowly in heart, and you will find rest for your souls. 30 For My yoke is easy and My burden is light."

Heavy laden are those who are carrying more than they can bear. When it comes to loss, there is so much to emotionally carry. My friend, you were not designed to carry the load alone. Jesus says to give it to Him and He will take it. When we give it all to Jesus, we will find rest to our soul. Your soul is your mind, will, and emotions. Give it to Him, and you will rest. One can recognize depression in the very moment that we don't want to respond to God in any way, shape or form. If you do not want to take that step towards rest, my friend the author of confusion and depression is scripting your decision and it needs to stop! There is a rest for you and begins at the point when you can give your loss, your hurt, your disappointment to Him by faith.

Another word for rest is the word peace. Look what Jesus tell his disciples to expect once He is gone, and they are dealing with His loss in their lives. He told them in **John 14:27 (NKJ)**
"Peace I leave with you, My peace I give to you; not as the world gives do I give to you. Let not your heart be troubled, neither let it be afraid."

Jesus literally is saying to each and every one of us. "Don't be confused about this, don't be troubled. I give you a peace and a rest as you release the loss and the pain to me." Now, it is very true that we would rather have our loved one back! We don't just want peace, we want our loved one back. The hard reality for us to face is that we will not get them back. You see the question of "What Now?" Will not be satisfied until we realize that they are gone. We settle it and now we receive the peace that He releases into our lives. We don't know exactly how it unfolds, but it does. You can't explain it. You can have peace and rest that will allow you to have a sound ability to make decisions. Find rest, and if you are unable to do that, then my friend, depression is speaking louder than your God. It is at this point you must admit that you need help.

If you find yourself lashing out at people for no apparent reason, then it is obvious that depression is beginning to set in. We are going to deal with anger in the next chapter, but for our discussion right now, we must recognize that unchecked and unrepented anger is a sign of depression. If you have to lash out at people, something is wrong. Recognize it and give grace to people! They don't always know what to do or to say. They are simply making every attempt to help and to serve. It is okay to be angry, but don't let it be prolonged. In various seasons, others will be hurt, and you will be hurt even more.

There are more symptoms of depression, but the ones that I have outlined for you are the foundational symptoms to look at. If depression is evident, don't stay in that arena. Get out of it! If you don't, things will not change. You will not be able to see clearly. You will not take the necessary steps towards healing and restoration.

You **cannot** do this alone, so stop trying. It hasn't worked thus far, and it will not suddenly start now. You must seek pastoral counseling and professional counseling. You cannot, nor were you designed to walk through this alone. God has put wonderful people and an incredible tool at your disposal. Allow the local church to help you and resource you to the place of health and emotional healing. It is the reason God established it here on earth, so please reach out and allow it/us to do our job. And that job is to help pull you through, out and beyond.

Right now, as you read this and find yourself identifying with an area of confusion and depression, this is what you need to do immediately:

First, change what you are meditating upon. The word *meditate* in the Bible means to dwell on and think deeply about. In the Hebrew, the word *meditate* means to speak and mutter. So, to meditate on the Word of God day and night, we speak it and mutter it to ourselves over and over again. Why is this so important? Because when you do this, the Author and Finisher of your faith becomes a reality to you. When you don't, and confusion and depression begin to set in, there is nothing to oppose them. It is at those moments wrong thought patterns develop. Stop working against God and begin to work with God by meditating on the His Word. When you do this, the author of confusion cannot be heard, because the Word of God is ringing in your ear. So, first, meditate on God's Word. Watch the peace and rest of the Lord begin to surround your life. Watch the situation and circumstances in your life begin to make a shift towards healing and restoration.

Secondly, to stop confusion and depression from entering into your life, and stop the flow of restoration, begin to get yourself involved in a small group of friends. The kind of friends that will support you by the Word of God and not the things of this world. That is who you need around you immediately. Those who will help you speak the Word of God when you don't feel like it. There will be many of those types of days when you can't, but others can do it for you. You need support! You need the local church. If your local church is not doing that for you, then do two things: (1) Make sure they know! That is right, they may not know what you are facing and what you are dealing with. Let them know. They do not know unless they are aware. Many people say, well they should know. They may not! Do not put unrealistic expectations on your church leadership. They are ministering and loving on many people and they simply do not know until you tell them. (2) You go to the ministry teams and elders of your church. The bible clearly tells us to call upon the elders when you are sick. My friend, if you are fighting depression and confusion is speaking loud in your life, you need to be cared for. You need to receive faith filled ministry. Your church can do that for you. If it can't then find another church that is ready to minister to your life. You go! You initiate it! There is a powerful church of Jesus Christ ready to love you and minister to you. Do those two things immediately.

Thirdly, take the super human exterior off and let people in. Until you become real with the place you are in, nothing is going to change. God cannot do for you what you are not willing to give Him. There must come a time where you can come before God and allow Him to release ministry into your life, your hurt, and your loss. We read it earlier in the chapter and I refer to it again.

Matthew 28:11- 10 (NKJ)
"Come to Me, all you who labor and are heavy laden, and I will give you rest. 29 Take My yoke upon you and learn from Me, for I am gentle and lowly in heart, and you will find rest for your souls. 30 For My yoke is easy and My burden is light."

Nothing happens until you come! You must take the step! Stop waiting on everyone else. God is waiting on you! My friend, if confusion and depression are eating away at your everyday life, you can see that change. It begins with you taking the steps to change who the author is. To change what is speaking into your life and what you are meditating upon every day. When you change that, God responds, and healing begins its process **in** you and **around** you. You will find rest and peace in your life.

In the midst of facing loss there are so many times, especially if one has lost a spouse, that the road is so difficult and hard. We say this all the time and it is very true, "People should not have to endure the loss of a spouse." We say that, but it happens to thousands every day across the globe. It is a part of life that is terrible, and we don't always understand it or why it does happen. In many cases the most used statement that keeps people confused about where they are and fighting thoughts of depression is because of this one question that weighs so heavy upon their heart. "Could I have done more?" The answer is always the same, "Yes!" Absolutely you could have done more. I could have done more! We all can do more!   What makes this so difficult is that we allow the pondering of that question to linger in our thoughts. As that thought lies there, the author of confusion and the open door to depression begins to open itself up to one's soul. Answer that question quickly. The answer is yes. You could have done more.

We can always love more, do things more healthily, pray more, worship more, serve more! We can and could always do more! But now, please shift from the confusion and the questioning of "Could I have done more?" to meditating on His Word. Do not entertain the author of confusion. Get around people that minister into your life and encourage you to find rest and peace in the Lord. The pathway is so difficult, do not make it more difficult than it should be.

Today answer the question "What Now?" Answer it by declaring unto your own heart and your own thoughts. What Now? God is with me! What Now? I will meditate, speak (over and over again) that the peace and rest of God is upon my life. What Now? No more confusion that makes way to depression. I have an author to my Faith and it is Jesus and His infallible Word. What Now? I should have done more! Yes, you should have, but so should the one who is gone from your life. Do everything you can today to put people in your life that speak into your heart and help establish the right-thinking patterns. God has you and He has not forsaken you! He is your comfort, your peace, and your rest!

Out of the Ashes *Chapter 19* – The Enemy to Restoration

I want to take you through a foundational journey into restoration. The reason that I use the term "journey," is because that is what restoration is...a journey. It is not a sprint. It does not happen overnight, and can take days, weeks, even months to years. You may say, "Thanks a lot for the encouragement." Before you let the voice of discouragement set in, remember the take away from the last chapter. Never allow yourself to take residence and settle in a place of unhealth. You must move forward and taking steps toward moving forward, will release you from where you are held. Those steps forward will move you into the place God has for you. That place is restoration. First, let's get the picture and image in our heart of where restoration comes from:

Psalm 23:3 (NKJ)- *"He restores my soul; He leads me in the paths of righteousness For His name's sake."*

Psalm 80:3 (NKJ) - *"Restore us, O God; Cause Your face to shine, and we shall be saved!"*

Jeremiah 30:17 (NKJ) - *"For I will restore health to you and heal you of your wounds,' says the Lord......"*

Job 42:10 (NKJ)- *"And the Lord restored Job's losses when he prayed for his friends. Indeed, the Lord gave Job twice as much as he had before."*

God is the Restorer of all that is empty, He is the Restorer of all that is missing, He is the Restorer of all that has been taken, and He is the Restorer of what we feel has been stolen out of our lives. God, and only God, can restore unto our lives what has been lost. Here is the key for each of us to grasp: We must respond by faith in the promise of "Who" God is. He is the Restorer! My response to God is to trust in His infallible Word.

The most powerful example of this is found in the book of Ruth. I encourage you to open your Bible and read this book. It is the picture of the restoration of God when it comes to the loss of life. Ruth's husband had died, and only her mother-in-law, Naomi, is left in the family.   She travels with her mother-in-law back to her home country. While working in the fields, she is noticed by a man of great wealth named Boaz, who was God's restoration to Ruth. What I want you to see is this powerful and yet foundational truth to restoration. God does restore! What we see in Ruth's life is that she kept her faith and stayed active. When it came to her loss, she kept moving forward. She committed to the journey.

Faith is information that you act upon. When there is an **active** faith in God as the restorer, restoration will come. I have learned this in my own personal journey of restoration. God desires to work with you and not against you.   What do I mean by that? When you and I respond like Ruth, we are entering the journey of restoration. It did not happen overnight, but in a short amount of time, Ruth began to see what God was bringing to her. She stayed active in her faith and with her life. James calls that work! James chapter 2 is outline of what we are discussing:

James **2:18 -24 (NKJ)** *"18 But someone will say, "You have faith, and I have works." Show me your faith without your works, and I will show you my faith by [g]my works. 19 You believe that there is one God. You do well. Even the demons believe—and tremble! 20 But do you want to know, O foolish man, that faith without works is dead? 21 Was not Abraham our father justified by works when he offered Isaac his son on the altar? 22 Do you see that faith was working together with his works, and by works faith was made perfect? 23 And the Scripture was fulfilled which says, "Abraham believed God, and it was accounted to him for righteousness." And he was called the friend of God. 24 You see then that a man is justified by works, and not by faith only."*

You see faith is corresponding action. The journey of restoration is you and I becoming active in moving forward. Many of us have heard or read the story of Job in the Bible. If you haven't, let me give you a spoiler, Job lost everything! In the end God restored it all back to Job and he possessed more than what he did before his loss. Job is an incredible story of God's restoration following tremendous loss and devastation. The powerful element is not just the end of the story, but Job's response along the way. Every one of his friends, and even his wife at one point told Job to curse God and die. You know it's a bad day when your wife tells you to give up and die. But Job did not stop believing in His God, he continued to put faith into action and trust the Almighty. Again, my friend, please let this drop into your heart. God is the Restorer of all, and He desires to work with you and in you. Your role is to put faith into action so that you do not get detoured on the journey of restoration.

In both of these examples, tremendous loss was felt. Both had experienced every form of loss. Restoration for Ruth was a husband and security once again in her life. For Job, God restored all land, livestock, and joy for living. If you have lost children due to an unfortunate sickness or accident, God can restore your joy, your love for life, your faith, and your hope.   We are not just talking about bringing something back, restoration is being built. We are also not taking about replacing loved ones. We can never replace the individual.   Restoration does not mean replacing. Restoration from God's perspective is making you better than what you were before and during the loss.

As a parent you may be saying, "Now hold on! How can God make it better by me not having my child?" I did not say it would be better without your child, I am saying that you will be better. God takes the pain of the loss and molds you into a better, merciful, and giving individual. Because of the pain you have endured, He restores to you an enduring faith and hope that this is not the end. Your experience God is going to use to help others in a time of need. He restores to you hope, confidence and peace in the day that you live in. It is not about replacing. It is all about restoring in you what you have lost due to your experience. When we talk about the journey of restoration, we are talking about what God is doing in you, to build and replace what you may have lost in your family's loss. God and only

God can restore you and rebuild what has been taken and create new in you and for you.

In order for you and me to stay on this journey of restoration, we must deal with the enemy of restoration. The enemy of your restoration is unforgiveness. Honestly, this is a powerful enemy to your ability to move forward on your journey. Unforgiveness will cripple you emotionally and exhaust you mentally. I do not know where the following phrase originated. I have been using it for years, because it is so true. I want to give someone credit for it, but I simply do not know who, because I have used it for such a long time. "Holding unforgiveness in our life is like drinking poison and expecting someone else to die". Unforgiveness is like a prison to your emotional and mental health. You will not move beyond where you are until this enemy is removed, and you are healed from unforgiveness.

Countless times I have been with families that could not bring healing to their lives because of their unwillingness to forgive and let go. I have sat bedside in the last minutes of life and watched people still hold onto certain things and say, "I just can't let go of what they did." We must stop immediately and forgive quickly. Jesus Christ and the powerful redemption that is in His sacrificial blood covers our sin and iniquities. When His blood is applied to unforgiveness by faith, it is cleansed and made whole. When you and I repent, He is faithful and just to forgive us of our sin.

When we receive communion, we are receiving what Jesus provided for us: the cleansing power of the blood of Jesus. In this journey of restoration, we must apply the only cleaning power of forgiveness. It is Jesus and the blood that was spilled out for our sin. Communion is a discipline of our faith in Christ, that is exercised by faith. When you repent of unforgiveness towards others, you are forgiven. You are justified and cleansed made new. I am being adamant on this point, because over the years I have counseled so many people and this foundational step helped them to restoration. It is not just my conviction, but it was Jesus's conviction has well.

Look at this: **<u>Matthew 18:21 -35 (NKJ)</u>** *21 Then Peter came to Him and said, "Lord, how often shall my brother sin against me, and I* *forgive him? Up to seven times?" 22 Jesus said to him, "I do not say to you, up to seven times, but up to seventy times seven. 23 Therefore the kingdom of heaven is like a certain king who wanted to settle accounts with his servants. 24 And when he had begun to settle accounts, one was brought to him who owed him ten thousand talents. 25 But as he was not able to pay, his master commanded that he be sold, with his wife and children and all that he had, and that payment be made. 26 The servant therefore fell down before him, saying, 'Master, have patience with me, and I will pay you all.' 27 Then the master of that servant was moved with compassion, released him, and forgave him the debt. 28 "But that servant went out and found one of his fellow servants who owed him a hundred denarii; and he laid hands on him and took him by the throat, saying, 'Pay me what you owe!' 29 So his fellow servant fell down at his feet and begged him, saying, 'Have patience with me, and I will pay you all.' 30 And he would not, but went and threw him into prison till he should pay the debt. 31 So when his fellow servants saw what had been done, they were very grieved, and came and told their master all that had been done. 32 Then his master, after he had called him, said to him, 'You wicked servant! I forgave you all that debt because you begged me. 33 Should you not also have had compassion on your fellow servant, just as I had pity on you?' 34 And his master was angry and delivered him to the torturers until he should pay all that was due to him. **35** "So My heavenly Father also will do to you if each of you, from his heart, does not forgive his brother his trespasses."*

Do you see the power in this foundational step to remove the enemy of restoration? You must forgive! Do it quickly.

What I have discovered in people's lives who get detoured in the journey of restoration is, they hit a road block and cannot move forward due to unforgiveness. In the case of the loss of a loved one, where do they get held up? Great question. People get held up on their journey because they can't forgive themselves for not doing more and not saying what needed to be said before their loved one passed. People get held up because they can't forgive others that may have done something to them in the midst of loss. People get held up by not forgiving the person that is gone. Let's pause right here for just a moment. This is very huge for people to face and to deal with.

Friend, if you are at a place where you cannot forgive the person who is gone for leaving you, for making the decision to do what they did, you must determine to let them go and forgive them. If not, you are in a prison and you are locked down emotionally and mentally. If your name is not Ruth, it is now for this moment. Don't stop! Continue on to your restoration journey. Apply faith, get to work and watch God restore to you what you have lost.

For you parents who may be reading, and you say, that is good for those who have lost a spouse but not for me. Wait a minute Ruth, I am still changing your name for this moment. You may not have lost a spouse, but I have encountered many parents who are so angry at what happened in the loss of their children that they are carrying unforgiveness. Don't get detoured. Stay on the journey, and God will restore your hope, your joy and your love for life. He will do it! Please don't get detoured.

Here is a major point of contention for most people: forgiving God. That is right! So many people, in the midst of loss, become angry at God for taking their loved one. If you are still reading this book, then you are growing in an understanding of who God is, and where God was in the midst of your loss and tragedy. I am very proud of you. But please, in this moment, forgive God! He is your answer to restoration, so please don't put God as your enemy! Forgive Him and watch the peace of God that will flow in your life by the Holy Spirit.

Please take a moment and do this. Put the book down and begin to repent for where you have held unforgiveness toward others, toward the one who is gone, toward yourself and even toward God. Pray, right now, "God, forgive me for holding unforgiveness toward.........and fill in the blank." Go on and pray, "God I forgive ....fill in the blank, in the Name of Jesus!"   That is how simple faith in action is. That simple prayer defeated the enemy to your restoration. I make this a habit every day in my prayer life. God, I forgive! I do it quickly, because I know that my restoration is at hand. Don't be your own enemy to the journey of restoration.

I also want to add another element to why this is so important. Unforgiveness is where anger builds. Unforgiveness is like a breeding ground for anger. Anger always needs a place to grow. When you forgive quickly, anger has no place to build. Now, understand that anger is a part of the grieving process.   Again, if it lingers too long then we are opening our lives up to the spirit of grief and our journey has just developed another enemy to our restoration.

The bible says in the book of **Ephesians 4:26- 27 (NKJ)** *"26 Be angry, and do not sin": do not let the sun go down on your wrath, 27 nor give place to the devil."*

It is okay to be angry, but that anger must have a termination date. If we allow the sun to go down, and we sleep on that anger, we are giving place to the enemy. The enemy will wreak havoc in our lives if we do not deal with our anger. When forgiveness flows in our life, the breeding ground for anger does not exist!   There are so many times that we are asking God to take care of our anger in our hearts, and this issue of unforgiveness, when God is saying, "I have done it. My Son Jesus had provided all that you need. Just apply what He has provided, and you will be healed and restored." You see, my friend, the process involves you and your heart. It literally involves you opening the closet of your heart and letting it all be exposed. Nothing and I mean absolutely nothing is ever changed as long as it is hidden from the light. But when the Light of God's Word shines into the darkness of your heart, the enemy of your restoration is exposed and can be defeated.   Here is the thing: God will not do it without you.   Come on Ruth, Come on Job, don't get detoured on the road to your restoration. God is the Restorer of all, but you must recognize the enemy and stay on the path to restoration.

I know that we have presented this multiple times throughout the story, but it is true. You can't do this alone. To stay on the path of restoration, you must put people around you to help you recognize that you are acting out of anger. To help you see the possibility of holding something against someone else, or even your God, can be holding you captive, let me give you five steps that will assist you every day.

1. **Forgive quickly.** Jesus taught us how to pray, and in this manner, Christ told us to forgive us our trespasses and we forgive those who have trespassed against us. This is a daily thing for every person, no matter how long you have been living this thing called a Christian life. Every day, forgive and ask for forgiveness. It is a lifestyle of repentance and I tell you my friend, it defeats the enemy to your restoration.

2. **Check your anger before you go to bed.** Don't go to bed on your anger. If you do, the enemy will have place in your thought life and he must be defeated. Jesus already won the battle over the work of the enemy in your life. The enemy, satan himself, is a defeated foe. However, the spirit of this world is at work to bring defeat, to steal, kill, and destroy all that God is attempting to build in your life. Give him no place. Check your anger every day. It is okay to be angry, but don't sleep on it. If you sleep on it, it grows. It is an open door to the enemy of your restoration. Don't allow it! It is simple to do. "God take it! I release this anger to you and I trust that you will bring peace, wisdom and revelation to the steps I need to take next." That is it. That is the prayer! That is the starting place. I promise you my friend, if you will continue to keep your anger in check and pray for the Lord to make the difference in your life, He will!   He is your restoration. Don't allow anger to detour you!!

3. **Don't have Job's friends.** All of Job's friends, and even his wife was giving him counsel to just give up and that God hated him. Job did not have good friends. You need good friends around you. There is wisdom found in a multitude of counsel. Is your counsel working with God, or is it working with the enemy to your restoration? Just ask that question. If the answer is no, they are not helping, then get new friends! Get involved in a life-giving church that will love you and help encourage you to stay on the path of restoration.

4. **Put faith into action.** Faith is corresponding action. Take the steps that correspond with the Word of God. That is what faith looks like in action.   "If the Word of God says that He is my peace,

then I thank Him for His peace over my life." I just activated faith
and put God's Word into action on my behalf. "If the Word of God
declares that He is the Restorer of my soul, then I praise Him for
His restoration." Again, I just put faith into action. When you deal
with your anger, you are putting faith into action. When you
confess your unforgiveness towards others, you are putting your
faith into action. Ruth never stopped moving forward in her
journey of restoration. That journey put her before Boaz, and God
restored unto her what was lost.   Put faith into action by
responding to what the Word of God declares. Don't waver from
it! Don't allow yourself to leave it.

5. **Thank God for His Restoration in your life.** You have the
revelation of what God is doing in your life when, you can thank
Him for what He is doing, even when you don't see any changes.
That is right.   You know that you are on the journey of restoration
and you are defeating the enemy on the front lines of your battle,
when you can thank God, and nothing is happening. When you
have the ability to thank God in the midst of the storm the storm
will pass, and God is there.   When you can thank God for what you
can't see, but your heart is settled on what He is able to do. You
will be working in the field and then all of the sudden, Boaz walks
into your life. Thank God for His restoration and you will begin to
see it unfold. It may not happen overnight, and it will not happen
overnight. When it does come, it will be incredible!

This is not designed to be everything for you concerning your
restoration. It is foundational. It is a place to begin. I have watched
our family take these critical steps and it has been the spring board to
God restoring hope, joy, and a love for life in the midst of our losses. It
is because of this foundational step; the beauty has come out of the
ashes. God is able, and He is so, so good! Stay committed to the
journey.

When we face the physical loss of someone that is close to us, there is such an indescribable void. An empty space that we literally do not know how to fill. It is in that emptiness that we will make every attempt to fill it until we can discover some form of peace. We look for something, someone, or a substance to fill that empty space. In our story, every character attempted to fill the space. Some found it quickly, and some may not have ever found it. Naturally, we will all make the attempt to fill that space, some of us succeeding and some not. Right now, in this moment, as you read the words on this page, I want to challenge you to open your heart for the next few moments.

What if I told you that there is an element in your life that comes from God that can fill the emptiness you are carrying? He created it just for you. What if I told you that in this element, you could see such a flow into the very empty place of your life? Would you be willing to listen? Would you be willing to open your heart to the soundest advice that will allow you to be filled? Would you be open to the greatest sense of peace that you have ever felt? I am so glad that you have answered yes to the above questions. That is incredible! Seriously, God created a peace that flows into your life in the midst of the emptiest moments.

Jesus says this **John 14:27 (NKJ)** *"Peace I leave with you, My peace I give to you; not as the world gives do I give to you. Let not your heart be troubled, neither let it be afraid."*

These are the words of Christ prior to His death upon the cross. Peace is the element that God has created for the emptiness in your life. Everything changes when you hold a peace that heaven releases in your life. Notice that Jesus said the peace He gives is not like the world. My friend, a step towards the world in the midst of loss will cause deeper wounds in your life. A step of faith towards the peace of God will fill the void and unfold a flow in your life that says, it is going to be okay.

If you could create an understanding of the flow of peace in your life, wouldn't you do it? If you could begin to fill the vacancy in your life, and see the emptiness begin to fill up with life, wouldn't you do that? Of course, you would! God has created that peace, and through Jesus Christ it is provided to you. This principle of God's Word is so powerful that Jesus himself told those who were the closest to Him prior to His death, "My Peace I give you." If Jesus took a moment to tell those who were closest to Him that peace would be the element of healing for them, then we need to hear that for ourselves. If this is a healing element that God provides, then how do we walk in this type of peace? Together let's build this foundation into the fabric of our faith. Let's take a close look at why the peace of God is supernatural.

First, Jesus said He will give it to you. A peace that the world cannot give, but only Him. If Jesus is going to give you something, it is outside the natural working of things. He promised that during loss, His peace will be given. That should be enough right? I am not just going to leave at that, even though that should be enough.

The Apostle Paul scripts this **Colossians 1:19 - 20 (NKJ)-** *'19 For it pleased the Father that in Him all the fullness should dwell, 20 and by Him to reconcile all things to Himself, by Him, whether things on earth or things in heaven, having made peace through the blood of His cross."*

Notice specifically at the peace that comes through the blood of His cross. Everything that surrounds the cross of Christ is supernatural. The cross was not the end, but the beginning of everything powerful about our salvation in Christ. When the blood of Jesus flowed upon the cross, it was the covering for your sin and my sin. His blood was the purchase made for the ransom of our sin. At such a great cost, my sin was paid by Jesus. Because of His blood that was poured forth upon that cross that held Him, there is a peace that is now present. Because He settled the cost of death, hell, and the grave, there can be peace. Death could not hold Him, hell could not stop Him, and the grave could not bury Him! There is no victory in the grave but because of Jesus and all that He provided, there is victory found in Him. Peace comes through what Jesus has provided, and all that He has done.

Look at what <u>**Isaiah 53:5 (NKJ)-**</u> *"But He was wounded for our transgressions, He was bruised for our iniquities; The chastisement for our peace was upon Him, And by His stripes we are healed."*

Here, the chastisement for our peace is the penalty that was due to our sin. Our punishment for our sin was upon Jesus. Because He paid the price, I now have peace. Do you see it? The peace that Jesus gives you came through His atoning sacrifice, and because of that, you have peace. The peace of God is supernatural because of Jesus and what He has done just for you. It is a supernatural flow into your life, especially in the midst of loss. Expect the peace of God to come and fill the vacancy in your life.

This does not mean that it is easy, but when the peace of God creates a flow into the emptiness, there is this "awe" moment where one can breathe, a moment where one says, "Thank you for your peace O God!" It is present, it is for you right now and it creates a supernatural flow in your life. Let's continue to grow in the peace of God. <u>**Colossians 3:15**</u> (NKJ)- *"And let the peace of God rule in your hearts, to which also you were called in one body; and be thankful."*

Let the peace of God rule in your hearts. What a command that the Apostle Paul gives here. Let, that means you make the decision on who is going to rule in your loss. The peace of God needs to flow in every area of your life.   When you see peace as the supernatural flow that Jesus has provided you, then you have to receive it. That is right!   Just thank God for His peace and He will provide it unto you. He will give it as a divine and heavenly flow into your life.

The Bible tells us that one of the names of God is Jehovah Shalom, which means "the God of peace." It is who He is! Earlier we shared with you that God is love. That is who He is! When I discover that God is Love and He is peace then I begin to understand that I need Him. His love is supernatural, and His peace is supernatural, and it is the deepest desire of God that we respond to who He is!   He is Peace! Allow the flow of His peace to fill any vacancy that you have due to loss.   I promise you that when you do, vacancy will diminish, and pain begins to subside. There is just a peace that, even though our loved ones are gone, it is only for such a short amount of time, and I will see them again. Come on peace of God, begin to reign in every area of my life! Amen! God is Peace.   Let's create that flow of peace in our lives by the Word of God.

2 Corinthians 13:11 (NKJ) *"Finally, brethren, farewell. Become complete. Be of good comfort, be of one mind, live in peace; and the God of love and peace will be with you."*

Now understand that in order to become complete there is always a process. When things are complete in you and in your heart, there is a flow of peace. Look at how the Apostle Paul outlines this for us in 2 Corinthians 13. This outline is a flow of the peace of God in our lives. It begins with drawing comfort. Jesus told us in John 14 that He would send a comforter unto us. Who is our comforter? The Holy Spirit is our comforter! He is so good at it. The Holy Spirit bringing comfort to us is the very power of God at work in our lives. My goodness! See how much God is for you and what He has provided for you in the midst of loss! Everything that you have need of in the midst of the trial you are facing and the loss that tears away at your heart, God has you! He has provided for you!

To unfold this peace in your life, you must grow in your fellowship with the Spirit of God. This is found in the midst of your worship and prayer. Please don't let your church service be your worship. Wake up and be a worshiper in the midst of your pain and watch the precious Holy Spirit begin to comfort you and build a flow in your heart and life. My friend, this peace is a peace that only God can release in your life. In your worship and prayer, you will be positioned to see an incredible flow of peace come upon your life and surround you.

The next thing he told us to do is, "be of one mind." Very simply, get focused.   In the midst of loss your mind is going all over the place, with the decisions that have to be made, and the questions that are rolling around. Get focused! When you do, something happens, the peace of God will come. That is right, get focused! If nothing else just stop the racing of your mind and call out to God and watch His divine and holy peace surround your heart. Watch the flow of peace begin to fill the vacancy in your life.

Is it really that simple? Yes, it is, but it is still very difficult to walk out every day. Here is the question for you: Do you want peace, or do you want to stay empty? If you want peace, take the steps to create the flow that God is desiring to do in your life!

Lastly, He says, "live in peace." It is a choice of what you are going to pursue, it is your choice of how you are going to live. Choose peace. Choose the peace of God that Jesus promised to give you. Live it out! Do it over and over again. Worship and pray, get focused and get your thoughts in order. Live in peace and then do it all over again. Worship and Prayer! Get focused and get your thoughts in order. Live in peace! The peace of God is a supernatural flow in your life. Make way for it to move in every area of your life. Allow God to be who He is in your life. He is peace!

Romans 15:13 **(NKJ)** *"Now may the God of hope fill you with all joy and peace in believing, that you may abound in hope by the power of the Holy Spirit."*

Romans 15:33 (NKJ) *"Now the God of peace be with you all. Amen."*

Philippians 4:7 (NKJ) *"and the peace of God, which surpasses all understanding, will guard your hearts and minds through Christ Jesus.*

2 Peter 1:2 (NKJ) *"Grace and peace be multiplied to you in the knowledge of God and of Jesus our Lord,"*

2 John 1:3 (NKJ) *"Grace, mercy, and peace will be with you from God the Father and from the Lord Jesus Christ, the Son of the Father, in truth and love.*

God has made His peace so freely available to all of creation. The only way we exempt ourselves from walking in such a divine flow of peace, is if we walk away from it. If we choose to fill the vacancy and emptiness in our life with another substance, then we will never see the true peace of God at work in our lives.

Let me give you a powerful picture of what peace can do in your life.   In the gospel of Mark chapter four, the disciples of Christ are crossing the sea with Jesus in the boat with them. A storm began to build, and the winds became tumultuous. Jesus lay asleep in the boat and they woke Him. Keep in mind just for a moment, the storm is raging, the wind is knocking this boat around in the water, things were extremely hectic, and yet Jesus was asleep and at rest. When you walk in a flow of peace, even during the storm, you are at rest. After they wake Jesus from His rest, He stands and speaks to the storm saying/commanding, "Peace be still!" The very release of this supernatural work of heaven on His behalf, called "Peace," caused the storm to be still.

You see my friend the supernatural flow of peace can calm the natural storms that we will face. If you have lost someone dear to your heart, you are in a storm. Peace is given to you! Peace is at work! You may not be able to see how it is at work, but it is at work and the storm will calm itself when you use what Christ has given you. Peace! Peace! More Peace! When you see the fullness of that powerful picture of Jesus releasing that word and the storm becoming still, then you can see how God can use His peace to calm your storm.

The Anderson's had a choice, and that journey was not easy for everyone, but eventually they made it. They testify today of the peace of God.   The hundreds of families that have been helped by this ministry have found peace amid the trial, the tragedy, the crisis. The peace of God is a flow that is supernatural, and it fills the void and the emptiness is not as vast. We never forget, but for those of us that are still here, there is a flow of peace. It is so incredible and so powerful for our lives. We want to challenge you to stop and take a moment to simply worship. Take a moment in prayer and ask God to release His peace over your life. Get focused, shut down the racing of your mind, and look deeply with eyes of faith into the heart of God. You will see Him, and you will begin to sense the peace of God flow into your life. I promise you!   Not one time have I led people in this same moment and they told me it did not work. One hundred percent of the time they all say, wow!

God will meet you, if you are willing to meet Him.   He is ready to release His peace over your life, if you are ready to invite that flow.

The peace of God is not just a story for Bible stories to make you feel better. It is the real deal that reflects all Heaven has for you. Appropriate the blessing of peace into your life and you will see the beauty that God has for you. The step is yours to make. When you do make that step, get ready! I believe you will begin to see the beauty that is in the ashes.   You are on your way out of the emptiness that you feel.   Take the step and God will meet you with His Peace!

Losing a loved one is so difficult. It is a hard journey to navigate through every decision that has to be made. One of the major issues in healing and restoration following death is the struggle with tomorrow. We have stated earlier that it is vitally important to NOT move too quickly. It is a vital mistake to make decisions that are life altering following the death of a loved one. At the same time, it is not healthy to let things go for a long period of time without making decisions that need one's immediate attention. No one in such situations ever likes to have the conversation of tomorrow, next week, next month, and even next year. No one wants to talk about moving forward. The reality is that tomorrow is upon us, and it will happen. There are choices and decisions that have to be made, and someone cannot make those decisions for us.   There is a healthy way forward. We need to develop the biblical principles of God's word in our lives so that we move forward in a healthy way.

Forward Principle One: *Perspective.* Throughout the Anderson story we have eluded to this principle multiple times.   The temporal perspective says that everything is over, nothing will ever be the same again.   The eternal perspective says that this is not over, and things will be different, and understanding that God will restore. As He restores, it will be better than what we ever thought it could be. It will never be the same, but God's ability to restore and heal our brokenness is continually at work. Let's look at few things to lay a foundation for this principle to be activated and built into the fabric of our lives.

First, Jesus said in **John 14:1-2 (NIV)** *"Do not let your hearts be troubled. You believe in God; believe also in me. My Father's house has many rooms; if that were not so, would I have told you that I am going there to prepare a place for you? And if I go and prepare a place for you, I will come back and take you to be with me that you also may be where I am. You know the way to the place where I am going."*

This word "troubled," in its original form, means to be confused.   Jesus was saying to the people that were closest to Him,

"Don't be confused about what is taking place in my departure." Why is this so important to understand? It becomes very important to each and every one of us that Jesus, the Son of God, in His very last moments on this earth as the Son of Man, shares a principle concerning eternity. In this moment you need to get the picture of how this principle was released to those who were closest to Him. This conversation takes place following one of the most referenced moments in Christ's life on the earth.

The Last Supper builds for us an image of Jesus in a room with all of His beloved disciples. The image that so many are familiar with is Jesus setting around a table with all those in whom He was close to at what is referred to as the "Last Supper". Following this famous image, is a conversation about what is going to take place. Jesus's life was going to be made a sacrifice for the sin of man. In this moment, they realize that Jesus is about to depart. They don't like where this conversation is going.

Every one of us who have ever lost someone, this is a painful conversation to have. In fact, it can be so painful that it feels like our heart is being broken into a million pieces. Our emotions feel like they are being twisted into a tsunami of brokenness that can't be described. In this moment, Jesus said this, "Don't be troubled, don't be confused." Confused about what? Here is the simple answer. Don't be confused, this is only temporal. Jesus said, "I go to prepare a place for you." You see my friend, this is just temporal and if our perspective is held by the temporal, moment of loss, we will miss the beauty of the eternal.

"I will come for you and you will be with me" Jesus said. What an incredible perspective to hold. Actually, it is a foundational principle that we must embrace as truth. This is not forever. The loss, the pain, the emptiness, the grief is only temporary when our perspective is open to eternity.

I was with my grandmother in her very last moments on this earth. My grandma, Bernice Anderson was a mighty woman of God. A prayer warrior for our family and the church. She prayed for a lifegiving church to be established in our area. I don't know if she knew her grandsons would be the founders and pastors of that church she was praying for. She probably sensed it. She was a woman that exemplified a Proverbs 31 woman. Her beautiful heart and virtue will be embedded into our hearts forever.

In her last moments, after being not very responsive for a couple of days, she did something that was so amazing to me. We had just gathered to surround her as family to pray and cover her with the prayer of faith and peace of God to surround her. Everyone had left the room and it was just me and my beautiful Grandmother in that moment. As I held her hand, she opened her eyes and looked up at the ceiling. Then she looked at me with those beautiful eyes of love and compassion. Looking up again at the ceiling she said with tears in her eyes, "I see Bob." Bob was her son who died from a sudden heart attack. "I see Joe." Joe was a son-in-law who died from a battle with cancer. With tears flowing down her cheek, "I see Monte." In that moment, I thought I was about to see something so incredible. The peace of God just filled the room in a very tangible way. It was as if the presence of Almighty God just rested in that moment. A warmth filled the room that you cannot even begin to explain with human words. She closed her eyes and in just a few moments later, drew her last breath.

My friend, in that moment I realized the beauty of what Jesus was saying in John 14. Don't be confused. Don't be troubled. This is only temporal; the eternal is where our perspective should be focused. Think about it for a moment. Eternity is waiting on us! Heaven is the eternal presence of God, His Glory, and the fulfillment of all that is promised by salvation. Eternity is the place of rest and peace. It is ultimate of everything that you can imagine that is good, perfect, and holy. Eternity is awaiting each and every one of us. It is the place of no more pain, sickness, disease and no more brokenness. It is where we trade this mortal flesh into immortality.   The Bible declares in **Proverbs 12:28 (NIV)** *"In the way of righteousness there is life; along that path is immortality."*

Romans 2:7 (NIV) *"To those who by persistence in doing good seek glory, honor and immortality, he will give eternal life."*

Corinthians 15:53-54 (NIV) *"For the perishable must clothe itself with the imperishable, and the mortal with immortality. When* *the perishable has been clothed with the imperishable, and the mortal with immortality, then the saying that is written will come true: "Death has been swallowed up in victory."*

1 Timothy 1:10 NIV *"...but it has now been revealed through the appearing of our Savior, Christ Jesus, who has destroyed death and has brought life and immortality to light through the gospel.*

Eternity is a beautiful perspective to hold.   That is why, in moving forward, it is a basic foundation to bring forth healing to one's life.   Does this perspective initially help with the emptiness, the pain, and the grief?   Yes, it absolutely does!   When you hold this perspective then peace follows. I can't explain how.   It is above the natural, it is supernatural. The peace of God rests upon your heart, because you know that this is only for a moment and you will be reunited again.   Lift your eyes above the temporal things of this world, and gaze into the wonderful promise of eternity.

Again, at this moment as we have done throughout this story. I want to give you the opportunity to look into your own heart and your own life.   Are you prepared for eternity?   Jesus goes on to say in response to Thomas,

"Thomas said to him, "Lord, we don't know where you are going, so how can we know the way?" Jesus answered, "I am the way and the truth and the life. No one comes to the Father except through me." **(John 14:5-6 NIV)**. Eternity does require a reservation! That reservation is for those who have accepted Jesus as Lord.   Have you reserved your place in eternity? Have you declared Jesus as the Lord of your life?   Do you believe upon Jesus as the Lord of your life? If not, make that reservation today.   Open your life to the eternal perspective. Look beyond this temporary moment and life that you live. Eternity is waiting upon you.

Pray this today, "Jesus, I confess with my mouth and believe in my heart that you have been risen from the dead. Be my Savior and my Lord.   Forgive me for every wrong thing done and wrong thing said. Amen!" What a powerful prayer, and if you prayed that for the first time, don't wait! Don't hesitate!   Share with someone and get into a good, life-giving, biblically based church. You can't do this on your own. You need a community of faith builders around you! My friend move forward by holding an eternal perspective. Look to Heaven and you will see the Glory and Grace of God at work in your life.

Forward Principle Two: *Revelation.* When we receive the revelation of God's word it changes how we respond to the world we live in. Example: When we receive Christ as Lord, we change how we live. That is the fruit of our salvation and the regeneration of our soul. We don't do the things we used to do. We no longer think with a debased mind, but we think with the mind of righteousness. We do not allow the things of the flesh to drive our desire. Instead, as a born-again believer upon Christ, I am a new man. The old is gone. I am led by the Spirit of God. I am changed because of the revelation of who I am in Christ. Revelation is the revealed knowledge of who God is. An easier way to define revelation is that it is a better way to see. I see the way that God has designed a way of living, principle or promise. It is revealed to me. The light has come on!

In the next few moments as you read the biblical view of death, I pray that it becomes a revelation to you. I pray that it ministers to your sorrow and your grief. I pray that it helps and aids you as healthy way to move forward. Let's look at these biblical principles of loss and death, and may they become revelation to your heart. May a light come on and may you have a better way to see where you are headed.

Listen to what the Word of God declares, *"Precious in the sight of the Lord is the death of His saints.* **(Psalm 116:15 NKJ)**." In God's design and creation, He created us with an individual will. With that will, we can do and make any decision that we desire. Jesus talks about a wide and a narrow path. He brings to us an understanding that wide is the way that will lead to destruction and narrow is the way that leads to life. We have a path to choose, we have a way to live and we will choose that path all by ourselves and we can place blame on no one. The design is this: if you choose to accept Christ and live righteously before him, picking the narrow way that leads to life, then you will receive the promise of an eternal heaven. That is the simple creative design by the Almighty. Let's not complicate the design! As you choose to believe and live for Christ, then the fulfillment of the promise of your salvation is eternal life. When we leave this temporal state of our living and enter eternity, we are received by our Heavenly Father. That is why in God's design the "death" of His saints is "precious". An Eternal Heaven is where we are received by God and obtain the promise of eternal life.

When this becomes revelation to you, when the light switch is turned on, you see the beauty of heaven and beauty of being received by our Heavenly Father. When we can see that, then death is a precious and a beautiful moment for children of God. With that revelation of God's Word activated in our lives by faith, we can see something so beautiful unfold for a loved one.

For us, even though the major losses that we have experienced were so tragic and way too premature for us as the Anderson family, we see beauty in it. We see Monte, H.O., Austin and Mary plus other family members being received by our Heavenly Father. There is no guessing for us. There is no doubt in our heart or thoughts about the promise of Salvation for them. They have been received and are rejoicing in the Glory of God and in the eternal promise of Heaven. When you see that beauty, you realize that they stepped into something so wonderful. As children of the most-high God, they would not want to be anywhere else. In just a few moments compared to eternity, we will be reunited. It is a beautiful thing!

Get the revelation of God's love and the anticipation of a Heavenly Father wanting to receive you. That, my friend, allows the peace of God to continue to be at work in your life as you walk into restoration.

Look at what is described about our lives on this earth. *"…whereas you do not know what will happen tomorrow. For what is your life? It is even a vapor that appears for a little time and then vanishes away* **(James 4:14 NKJ).**" When we face tragedy and the loss of a loved one, we quickly realize that life is very fragile. The truth is this: we are very fragile beings that live in a broken world. At any moment for any one of us, the reality of this truth can be upon us. What changes is the revelation that thousands of people face this reality every day. We are not alone in loss, in tragedy, and in grieving. Our life and our very being is here today and gone tomorrow. The

Bible goes on to show us, *"… All people are like grass, and all their glory is like the flowers of the field; the grass withers and the flowers fall,* **(1 Peter 1:24 NIV)**."

Life grows and then it is no more.   The revealed knowledge is this, "We will all make a departure from this temporal life."   You are not in charge of how you entered this world and you will not be in charge of how you leave.   It will happen, and we need to be ready. Life is here today, but it can be gone tomorrow.

I believe this next illustration shows us that God expects us to move forward. Moses has just passed, and Joshua is being commissioned into leading Israel into the promise of that which God alone had promised them. This is what the Word of God says, *"Moses my servant is dead. Now then, you and all these people, get ready to cross the Jordan River into the land I am about to give to them—to the Israelites* **(Joshua 1:2 NIV)**."   This is God speaking about an amazing man. A tremendous leader and deliverer of the people.   "My servant is dead." That is it! That is all God spoke. His servant is dead, now go. Move forward into all that I am providing unto you. This is a powerful revelation.   Get ready for it!   The promise is still there for Joshua, even though the only friend, and spiritual leader that he had was gone. God told Joshua to move into the promise. God's view is this: His servant has been received into Heaven, Moses is not going to do anything else in the earth. God is saying, "I still need you Joshua. Moses is okay, in fact Moses is doing incredible. I need you to move into the promise."

My friend, right now you may have lost someone you dearly love. They have been received into the Glory of Heaven. You now need to fulfill the promise. Get after it and move forward into what God specifically has for your life. What a powerful revelation this is for our life. God says, "Move forward, I still have promise for you and purpose for you. I still have a plan that is at work for you. Move into that promise."   You see, this revealed knowledge of how God views what has taken place unfolds for us that we are not yet done. If we are still drawing breath, then there is a promise that awaits. Move forward into it!

When the light comes into your heart by revelation of God's Word and God's design, then you understand that it is okay to move forward. You still have a promise to be fulfilled. It is waiting on you! Even though who you are on the journey with has changed, it is still for you. I believe with every ounce of who I am, God would whisper to you, "I have received them and now you fulfill the promise that is for you." I can look and see them by faith in heaven, at rest and in His Glory. I am running my race of faith to join them one day. Let the revelation of God's Word come alive to you and you will move forward into your promise.

Forward Principle Three - ***New Normal.*** There is not one person that ever likes to change. Change is always a process of acceptance. To move forward into the restoration that God has for you, one must become accepting of the new things that are around them. It is not going to be the same. There will be a new normal that we have to grow into. In order to grow into your new normal, you must open up to new things and new people. Think about this for a moment, restoration means "new." Not only new, but better than what you thought it could be. In moments of loss, if we are not careful, we will get locked into an image that it can't be okay, and it will never be good like it was. We can't change what happened, but we can look and walk into the "new normal." Different is okay, and one will discover that there are things that you forgot that you enjoyed. Or even better, there are things that you will discover that you will enjoy.

To build this for you, I want to take you to the book Job in the Bible. I am going to focus on the end of his story. If you recall, he lost everything. Everything was gone but then God restored unto him and then some. It was different, and would have been a "new normal" for Job to walk in. Different livestock, more land and family that was added to him. All that he had lost, God restored, but it was different than what it was before. Job thought that he would never see the things that he had possessed before. If God did that for this character in the Bible, why would it not be possible for you? God specializes in brokenness, and He comes to restore and to rebuild broken places. It will be different, and it will require a "new normal". Practically, with this principle at play in your life, you need to do the following to help you move forward into the new normal for you.

1.   **Accept the new.** That is right, get used to new things and that everything you do in the journey will have some elements of new. That is okay! Embrace it and enjoy what God is bringing into your life. Recognize that God is at work and restoring to you what you have need of. Remember if He could do it for the character named Job, He can do it for you.

2.   **Discover the new.** You can't stay hidden and expect new to come. You can't ignore and close the door on new people and new things coming into your life. God will not restore to you what you are not open to receive by faith. In the Bible, James tells us that we have not because we ask not. Ask for the new, discover the new in people. Discover the new in things to do and places to go and see. When you discover the new, you are discovering the way forward. God will give you what you have need of in the hour in which you need it. You are going to have to get out. Don't allow yourself to stay hidden.

3.   **New People.** God uses people to produce healing in your life. Throughout the Word of God, you see this play out over and over. One specific example is Naomi and Ruth. Ruth lost her husband, who was the son of Naomi. Naomi took Ruth into her own home, loved her, cherished her, and brought her to a place of healing. It was Naomi that introduced Ruth to Boaz. Boaz was the new for Ruth that restored so much unto her life and to her individual journey.

Open up to new people coming into your life. New friends and new relationships that are God centered and righteous in the fruit of their own lives, can be used of God to help and to aid you in moving forward. Open up and watch and see who God sends into your life.

4.   **Community of Faith.** A new normal for you may be a new community of faith. You home church is your hiding place and the refuge that you need in your journey. It may be very possible that a new ministry to serve in is the new normal that you need to move from where you are to a place of healing and restoration.

There is a man in our church that recently lost his beloved wife. His name is Mike. I had known Mike in the community for years. In this moment of loss, I was drawn to him.   They did not attend our church at the time, but I had the privilege of leading her service for Mike. We embraced him and have seen God do so much in healing the brokenness in his heart. We have seen him get involved in the life of our church and open up his life to a community of faith. A new normal for him was to come to our outreach ministry and simply help. He moves things and helps our ladies as he can. That new normal around a community of faith has helped him move forward in healing and restoration. He came, and he opened up to a new normal of people and serving. In return, he has seen a loving church family embrace him and support him in a way that he never thought possible. Start with the process and allow others to walk with you, don't shut people out.

Allow them to help you move forward. God has a plan for you. He has a plan that will move you forward into His promise. Move forward! Don't get stuck! God is still at work in every area of your life.

"Overwhelmed is a natural feeling when walking through the loss of a loved one." I have heard that statement multiple times. Not just in the midst of our own lives and loss, but also in ministry. Allow me to propose a thought, what if you could be overwhelmed by God instead of your circumstances... If you could, would you receive it? God specializes in taking the moments of your greatest pain and overwhelming you with His divine grace. The lowest points in your life are actually the launching points of God's grace to move in your life. Honestly, I can't tell you the number of times that we have been told as a family, "How much more can you take?" The answer to that question is, "no more!" We don't desire anymore loss or pain (no one does).

Here is something that will help you move from any level of pain or loss you are currently experiencing. When we began to recognize the overwhelming power of grace at work in our lives, it launched us into healing and restoration. Instead of becoming overwhelmed by what we were facing and dealing with, we began to recognize God's grace at work. We discovered a powerful reflection of God's love for us as we shifted from being overwhelmed by our circumstances to being overwhelmed by God's grace. It is for great reason that the song *Amazing Grace* is possibly one of the most familiar Christian choruses that exists. The grace of God **is** amazing! Words cannot even begin to do justice to the title, grace. Beyond what is familiar to us about grace is the empowerment that it brings to each and every one us. The grace of God is the ability to move from your circumstance into the plan and purpose of God. I like this definition of grace: "God moving on your behalf even though you do not deserve it." *There is someone that deserves the credit for that definitive statement of grace, I just don't remember who.* Let's bring some more understanding to that definition.

First, the Bible declares, ***"For it is by grace you have been saved, through faith—and this is not from yourselves, it is the gift of***

God." **(Ephesians 2:8 NIV) Grace**, by Greek definition means "unmerited favor." Salvation is a free gift from God. By grace you have been saved or received that gift. It is a free gift, it is unmerited, you do not deserve it, but God gives it to you. In other words, God chose to give it to you and you can do nothing in and of yourself to deserve it. You cannot be good enough, or perfect enough to receive it. Salvation comes to you by the powerful force of grace. Everything that God has provided to you comes by His Grace! We don't deserve it, and yet He still provides what we have need of. Grace changes everything. I have to repeat that. I do not want you to miss this life changing point. Grace changes everything! In fact, I am going to put it into all caps for you.

GRACE CHANGES EVERYTHING!

Think about it for a moment. Salvation comes to you by the avenue of grace. When you and I receive salvation and become born again, everything changes. We were once in darkness, but now through salvation, we are in the light of God's love and righteousness. We were once in sin, but now we are in righteousness. We were once totally lost, but now we are found. We were once bound by sin and hell, but now we are destined unto an eternal heaven. Everything has changed. God moved on your behalf and you did not even deserve it. The powerful force of grace works the same way in every area of your life. It changes everything! If we are in sorrow, everything **will** change by His grace. If we are bound by grief, everything **will** change! If we are confused in the process of our journey, everything **will** change! How are we going to walk this out? We are saved by grace through faith. Faith is the vehicle that transports God's grace into your life and circumstances. Faith is not just something that you do, but it is something that you know.

"Faith is the substance of things hoped for, the evidence of things not yet seen". **(Hebrews 11:1 NKJ)** Grace and faith ride together. Your faith, the substance of what holds you in the midst of the storm, when placed in God, will open your life to more of God's Grace. God loves to respond to faith. He has done it over and over again

throughout biblical history. The woman with an issue of blood pressed through the crowd and touched the hem of Jesus's garment. Jesus stopped, and the Word of God says that virtue left His body and she was made whole. What happened? She extended her faith to press through the crowd to get to Jesus. Faith was extended, and grace was released. She did not deserve it any more than the next person, but God responded to her faith and grace was released to her. We must take note of what Jesus said, "Your faith has made you well." Her faith moved heavens compassion, and the grace of healing was released to this woman. In one moment with Christ, she was overwhelmed by the grace of God. She did not earn it, but faith in operation opened up for grace to be released. Again, please don't forget that your salvation comes to you by grace, not deserved, but comes to you through faith.   Her faith opened up the opportunity to be overwhelmed by grace. That grace changed everything for that woman. Grace will change everything that you are currently facing.

In Mark's gospel, chapter 10, a man by the name of "Bartimaeus" did not have sight. He cried out, "Son of David have mercy on me!" Jesus responded to him and said, "Your faith has made you well." This man became overwhelmed by the grace of God because of faith, a substance in this man's heart that rose up within him caused him to pursue Christ. That faith became transportation for grace and he received healing. In Luke chapter 17, a man with leprosy comes to Christ and cries out to Him and says, "Have mercy on me?" Jesus responds and tells him, "Your faith has made you whole." Faith was activated, and grace was released. Again, and again, Christ was moved by the presence of faith and grace was released in an overwhelming way. People that we just mentioned, were never the same again. When you and I are walking through loss, so much changes. The grace of God is the powerful source of heaven that surrounds you. When your faith is placed in God and not anything else, grace will be transported to your life in an overwhelming way.

"And God is able to make all grace abound toward you, that you, always having all sufficiency in all things, may have an abundance for every good work." **(2 Corinthians 9:8 NKJ)**

Is it not incredible that God is able to make all grace abound toward you? That is a promise to you and I. All grace abounding toward us. This passage of scripture comes from 2 Corinthians 9, in the midst of a conversation about giving. Even though this is in a conversation on giving, we cannot miss the principle that is released. When we engage in giving, God responds with grace and He causes it to abound in our lives so that we have sufficiency for all our needs. What I want you to notice, my friend, is that we are involved. We are the givers. We are the ones who respond in faith, and then grace is transported to our situation.

You are involved in the process. Can I challenge you today to get involved? Don't sideline your life from the game of restoration. Get out on the field and be involved. Release your faith and trust that God **is** able to move on your behalf by His divine grace and change everything. It will not look the same, but it can be healed and restored better than what you could ever imagine.

Every character described in this book of the Anderson family walked out this principle of healing. They began to follow this principle and grace was transported to the most painful places of their lives. Everything changed, and they were overwhelmed by God's grace. They learned that faith and grace do ride together. Grace does abound when faith is activated. We must activate that faith and trust in God. I want to give you three practical ways to activate your faith so that grace will be transported to your circumstance, and the overwhelming presence of grace will heal, restore, and change everything!

1.	**Faith begins with the Word of God.** The only way faith grows in your life is by God's Word. The Word of God is the source for all power and authority on the earth. Your desire for God's Word will determine your desire to walk in faith. Every promise in the Word of God is **for** you and it is for the establishing of your faith in what God declares by His Word. Today, and every day, read the Word of God and watch how your faith will grow. Study God's Word and watch your understanding become fruitful. Memorize the promise of God's Word in the area of healing and restoration and you will grow in faith. It all begins with His Word. If you desire faith to transport grace, then grow in the Word of God.

2.	**Faith is what you know, more than what you do.** When you know that God desires to restore and to heal your life, then you are in faith. It is knowing deep within your heart that God is able to do what He has promised to do, that establishes your faith. Earlier we stated that Hebrews tells us, *"Now faith is the substance of things hoped for, the evidence of things not yet seen."* Faith is knowing, it is the substance of your heart and your thoughts that hold you in the middle of your storm. What is your substance? If it is people, then people are limited to their ability. If your substance is faith in God, then you are placing trust in that which is above the natural. If your substance is alcohol, then alcohol will only numb the situation and not change anything. Outside of faith, every other substance will leave you, not only with the same outcome, but with additional issues stacked upon it. What is your substance? If it becomes knowing God and knowing what His word declares over your life, then grace expands and changes everything.

3.   **Walk in thanksgiving.** This was the most difficult step for the Anderson family.   But once we all began to thank God that we were still here, when we began to thank God for the purpose that He has for us, when we began to thank God for the gift that we shared in Monte, H.O. Austin and Mary, faith began to expand.   When we learned to be thankful for what we were able to experience and what we still had, our faith increased and trust in God grew in our hearts.   When you can become thankful in the midst of your despair, my friend, get ready for grace to be transported to your life.

Everything is about to change!

*"Enter his gates with **thanksgiving** and his courts with praise; give thanks to him and praise his name."* **(Psalm 100:4 NIV)**

*"Give **thanks** to the Lord, for he is good; his love endures forever."* **(1 Chronicles 16:34 NIV)**

*"I will give **thanks** to you, Lord, with all my heart; I will tell of all your wonderful deeds." (Psalm 9:1 NIV)*

*"I will give you **thanks**, for you answered me; you have become my salvation."* **(Psalm 118:21 NIV)**

*"But **thanks** be to God! He gives us the victory through our Lord Jesus Christ."* **(1 Corinthians 15:57 NIV)**

When we learned as a family to give God thanks for His Grace at work in our lives and in the midst of such tragedy, everything began to change. Aubrey and Allie both stopped looking at what was lost and turned to a faith in God. They became people who were no longer drowning in despair but thanking their Heavenly Father for all that He was doing in their midst, and everything began to change.   We all were truly overwhelmed by the grace and presence of God at work in our everyday life.

So practically speaking, let's help you do this every day. That is right. Every single day you can be overwhelmed by the grace of God surrounding your life.   It is not just our encouragement but the encouragement of the Word of God. God is able to make all grace abound to you. Thank God today! You can do this. "God, I thank you for your Grace that is abounding in my life!" You are the one in charge of your faith.   No other person can do it for you.   If you are waiting on someone else to, then you will be waiting a long time.   God is waiting for you. He desires to abound and overwhelm you with His grace. Get the transport ready.   Get your faith established in His Word. Know it deep within your heart and be thankful. The grace of God is waiting for your response. Increase Grace and watch healing and restoration unfold. Overwhelmed by the grace of God is the moment when everything changes. The Anderson family is so thankful for all the restoration and changes that have unfolded in their lives.   No, it does not bring our loved ones back. What it does, however, is change everything around us so that we can be whole, healed, and restored. Stop looking around for answers and hope. Look to the Word of God and the Heavenly Father that is the Restorer of all. Build your faith and watch what grace will do on your behalf. Don't think about it anymore, just simply respond by faith and watch your Heavenly Father overwhelm your life with His Grace. Get ready everything is about to change!

Out of the Ashes *Chapter 23* – Heritage of Faith

At the beginning of this closing chapter, let's take a moment to reflect on the foundation of everything that has held the Anderson family together in some of the most difficult moments of our lives. Faith in God is our solid foundation!   We do not shy away from that and we do all we can to develop the Heritage of faith in the next generation.   That foundation began with Don and Carrol Anderson. Papa and Annie, we are all so thankful for you and the steadfastness of your faith in God.   The following are letters that are written to give thanks to Don and Carrol for all that they have done.

Dear Mom and Dad,
I cannot thank you enough for all your sacrifice and love for each of your children and grandchildren. You have endured an incredible amount of loss in your lifetime. In every tragic loss, I have watched you grieve. I have watched you cry until you have had no more tears left. I have watched you sacrifice time, money and even some dreams of your own to care for your grandchildren. I am so amazed by your strength and heart for your family. You have built a Heritage of Faith that will be forever remembered. Thank you for all you have done and all that you have given up. I love you more than words can ever express.   You both are my heroes.   With Love,

Cody and Amy

Dear Mom and Dad, Under **His Wings: Psalm 94:4**
I had watched my parents process the loss of their first born, their pastor, and their son, just a short time prior to losing my husband. We as a family had already asked all the questions as to why our faith, lack of faith, anger, and sadness. In many ways we may have been emotionally bankrupt when another loss came. In that moment they stepped up to walk their daughter through a different kind of loss.   To

my dad I want to say thank you for your strength and spirit of peace that you brought to me. A firm foundation where I could feel safe and secure as I processed the loss of my best friend and husband, as well as my children's hero. Your arms around me and your soft words of "I am so sorry." Even as you said that, you knew that there was nothing you could do to remove my pain. A parental struggle that we have for our children, was all I needed. There is a picture in the newspaper that is forever in my mind. The sheriff had handed to me the newly folded flag, and my father is sitting next to me with his arm engulfing me, surrounding me, comforting me. That is my "under His wings" moment. Sitting with me, just holding me securely, silent in that moment, with nothing that could have been said, or should have been said. Having just lost my brother drove home that understanding. I just needed you to be there. "Peace be still and know that I am God" became my resting place. I know in God's Word, He promises to protect us under His wings. If we are the Body of Christ then "Under His Wings" is where I rested, as my parents come to my side and covered me in their arms.   Mom, you were amazing. Nurturing and quietly seeing to my needs. Spending several weeks with me and my children as we tried to piece the puzzle back together without the center piece. Your patience, prayers and presence were such a blessing. Letting me go through the motions, finish redoing my home, building beside me, laughing and crying, sometimes at the same time. All of that allowed my spirit to heal.   The Holy Spirit comes as a teacher and a comforter and again, God used a mother to provide the care my spirit man needed.   Thank you both from the bottom of my heart for all you did, and continue to do for the family, and the family of God.

I love you Dedria

Dear Annie and Papa,

There are not enough words in the world to be able to describe how much I love you and how thankful I am that God chose me to be your granddaughter. There has never been a moment in my life that I ever questioned your love for me, even throughout all the trials and loss of our family. The unmovable, unshakable, unwavering faith that the two of you have had and shown throughout my whole life has been awe inspiring and something everyone in this world could use a little dose of. That faith does not just stop with Jesus but continues with people as well, and one of those people being myself. I lost my way for a while, but your faith and sacrifice to take me in completely changed my whole world and that is something I will never be able to repay back. I watched you sacrifice a lot over the years and take in my brothers and me at different times in our lives because we just needed a whole lot of love, Jesus and a calm place within the storm of life to rest. It is so humbling to watch the two of you and know that there is not a single thing you would not try to do for myself or the rest of our family if you could. You have built a legacy within this family that will last generations to come because of your faith in the Lord, your sacrifices for your kids and grandkids, and the unconditional love you have shown all of us throughout our entire lives. I can only hope that the legacy Kolton and I build together in this life is even a fraction of the one you have built throughout all these years. You made me a better person, and in different ways, you have made all your grandkids better people. Each one of us has had an amazing example of the type of person we all want to strive for and be. We all have a beautiful example of how we want to be in our marriages because of the example you set before us. Your faith, your sacrifice, and your legacy will never go unnoticed. Now all I can say is thank you for everything, I know that isn't enough and it never will be, but I love you with all my heart and I thank God every day that he made you mine.

Love, Allie

Papa and Annie,
I am so thankful for you both. You have always been a pillar of faith for this family and you continue to show us about love and righteousness. Your marriage and love for each other is almost unheard of these days and it's a testament of faithfulness. I couldn't be here today without you both. Papa, you have always shown me that when you work hard and show character that it pays off every time. Also, your stories and life lessons are full of wisdom and humor (mostly humor). I realized the other day I have only seen you cry a handful of times and I know it's because you show strength when everyone needs you to be strong. When we lost dad, you stepped up and walked in a role that was not meant for you, but you did it with excellence.

Annie, I thank God for you all the time. You prayed for me and stood in the gap when I was running from Him. You have always been a warrior for this family and always go after the prodigals. You speak life into situations where there doesn't seem to be an upside, and press into God in all things. You taught us that battles are won on your knees in prayer, and that with God all things are possible. You have always been a no-nonsense person and I am always full of nonsense. The back and forth talks we have, I truly enjoy. Especially when you give me the look that says "Aubrey James, you better straighten up."

I am forever thankful of the example that you both show your family on a daily basis of what it looks like to follow Jesus. It is possible that I don't tell you enough but, you both have been amazing role models. I am proud to be an Anderson! The number one ministry a man and woman have is their family. You have done that in an excellent way.

I love you both to the moon and back,

Aubrey

A heritage is not something that happens by accident. A strong heritage is built on the foundation of something and then instilled into the next generation. The heritage of the Anderson family is established on the rock of our salvation, Jesus Christ. In all that we do as a family, we strive to reflect the character and righteousness of Christ. Are we perfect in it? Absolutely not! But we strive for it every day of our lives. The next generation is carrying the torch and our heritage of faith is being established for years to come. The Apostle Paul said it best when he said, *"Not that I have already attained, or am already perfected; but I press on, that I may lay hold of that for which Christ Jesus has also laid hold of me."* **(Philippians 3:12 NIV)**

We press on, "Out of the Ashes" of our tragedy and into the victory that is Christ. We have risen above our loss only by the Grace of God. Our loss has had a major impact on our hearts and minds. Today, we carry on the heritage of faith that was the anchor to our soul. As you complete this story, it is our prayer that you continue strong in yours. Take a close look at yourself and your family. Is there an evident heritage of faith being built in your home and family? Do you see what it is that you desire to see in your home? If the answer to these questions is no, then let's begin a powerful journey of changing and building that heritage.   My friend, this is a long journey, not a sprint.   In the concluding moments of this story let me help you build a heritage of faith that can bring any family out of the tragedies of this world and live a full life.

First: Get your family into a life-giving church. In your city or in your community, is a church that is full of life.   You need to find a place to plant yourself so that you and your family can flourish.   We cannot do this thing called life, without others.   You cannot walk and run the race of life without people around you. You need a church that releases faith and relevant messages to your everyday life. If you have children, they need all the framework of faith that they can receive. You have the responsibility to put the Word of God into them so that when they grow old, they will not depart from it.   Find a great church and get involved.

Second: Lead your home according the Word of God, not the influence of the world.   You don't have to be perfect, but if your children see you in prayer and making quality decisions, then they know what to do.   Your decisions must be based upon the Word of God and the leadership of the Holy Spirit.   When they see you lead in that manner, they will follow. They will always remember what was modeled before them.   Use your house as a light of God's Word and you will see a heritage established that will carry the next generation.

Third: Love like God loves.   That is right, love like God loves. Unconditional is the love of God.   It keeps no record of wrongs and it is not haughty and puffed up.   It is a genuine love that does not judge or condemn, but it does produce life.   When you love beyond yourself, you begin the process of building an incredible heritage for your family to follow.   Love with strength and compassion.   A strength that holds one another accountable, and a compassion when people in your home need mercy.   We all have issues, challenges and struggles in our family, however, the Love of God chases people down.   The Love of God draws people to the place of change. When the Love of God is present, people are drawn to change.   When you love, your heritage of faith is strong, and does not blow away during a storm.

These steps are so simple, but it takes a lifetime to walk out. So, when you close this book for the final time, I pray the challenge is accepted to build a heritage of faith for the next generation.   Focus on it! Lead your family with that at the forefront of all that you do.   The next generation needs an example and I believe that example is you. Continue your course and walk in the best of what God has in store for your life.   He has your best interest in mind, and He is for you.   Follow all that God has for your life.   Not just at the end of your life, but every day that you draw breath.

Every day walk in the beauty and the power of the "Good News" of your salvation. I want to conclude with **Isaiah 61:1 – 3 (NKJ)** *"The Spirit of the Lord God is upon me, Because the Lord has anointed Me to preach good tidings to the poor; He has sent Me to heal the brokenhearted, to proclaim liberty to the captives, and the opening of the prison to those who are bound; To proclaim the acceptable year of the Lord, and the day of vengeance of our God; To comfort all who mourn. To console those who mourn in Zion, **to give them beauty for ashes,** the oil of joy for mourning, the garment of praise for the spirit of heaviness; That they may be called trees of righteousness, the planting of the Lord, that He may be glorified."*

Build such a heritage of faith in your life and home, that when trials, crisis, and even loss come, you are expecting the God of all comfort to give you beauty in exchange for the ashes.   You will be restored. You will be healed. You will be able to move forward, "Out of the Ashes".

CPSIA information can be obtained
at www.ICGtesting.com
Printed in the USA
LVHW080236150119
603872LV00002B/3/P